D1526439

A Student's Guide to

EMILY
DICKINSON

Titles in the **UNDERSTANDING LITERATURE** *Series*:

A Student's Guide to
EMILY DICKINSON
0-7660-2285-4

A Student's Guide to
F. SCOTT FITZGERALD
0-7660-2202-1

A Student's Guide to
NATHANIEL HAWTHORNE
0-7660-2283-8

A Student's Guide to
WILLIAM SHAKESPEARE
0-7660-2284-6

A Student's Guide to
JOHN STEINBECK
0-7660-2259-5

A Student's Guide to

EMILY DICKINSON

Audrey Borus

Enslow Publishers, Inc.

40 Industrial Road	PO Box 38
Box 398	Aldershot
Berkeley Heights, NJ 07922	Hants GU12 6BP
USA	UK

http://www.enslow.com

Copyright © 2005 by Audrey Borus

Library of Congress Cataloging-in-Publication Data

Borus, Audrey.
    A student's guide to Emily Dickinson / Audrey Borus.— 1st ed.
        p. cm. — (Understanding literature)
    Includes bibliographical references and index.
    ISBN-10: 0-7660-2285-4
    1. Dickinson, Emily, 1830-1886—Handbooks, manuals, etc. 2. Women and
literature—United States—History—19th century—Handbooks, manuals, etc.
3. Poets, American—19th century—Biography—Handbooks, manuals, etc.
I. Title. II. Series.
PS1541.Z5 B555
811'.4—dc22

                                                                    2004018098
ISBN-13: 978-0-7660-2285-0

Printed in the United States of America

10 9 8 7 6 5 4 3 2

To Our Readers:
We have done our best to make sure all Internet addresses in this book were active
and appropriate when we went to press. However, the author and the publisher
have no control over and assume no liability for the material available on those
Internet sites or on other Web sites they may link to. Any comments or suggestions
can be sent by e-mail to comments@enslow.com or to the address on the back
cover.

Illustration Credits: Amy Paulson Herstek, pp. 26, 91, 120; Archives
and Special Collections, University of Nebraska-Lincoln Libraries, pp. 45,
122; Emily Dickinson Museum: The Homestead and the Evergreens, p. 12;
Enslow Publishers, Inc., p. 109; Library of Congress, pp. 15, 104, 111;
Photo by Frank Ward, courtesy the Dickinson Homestead and the Trustees
of Amherst College, pp. 47, 49; Reproduced from the *Dictionary of American
Portraits*, published by Dover Publications, Inc., 1967, pp. 24, 30, 43, 52,
102, 116, 118.

Cover Illustration: Library of Congress (inset); Photo by Frank Ward,
courtesy the Dickinson Homestead and the Trustees of Amherst College/
Corel Corporation/ Hemera Technologies, Inc. (background objects).

CONTENTS

1 I'm Nobody—Who Are You?
An Introduction to the Life and Works
of Emily Dickinson 7

2 How to Read a Poem
Understanding the Poetry of Emily Dickinson 34

3 I Heard a Fly Buzz
Death and Eternity in Dickinson 55

4 Tell All the Truth
Truth, Faith, and Reality in Dickinson 74

5 A Certain Slant of Light
The Natural World in Dickinson 88

6 War
The Influence of the Civil War on Dickinson 100

7 There Is No Frigate Like a Book
The Legacy of Emily Dickinson 114

Chronology 126

Chapter Notes 129

Glossary 138

Selected Poems
by Emily Dickinson 142

Further Reading 148

Internet Addresses 149

Index 150

I'M NOBODY— WHO ARE YOU?

An Introduction to the Life and Works of Emily Dickinson

Imagine someone so shy you never see her, someone who guards her privacy so fiercely that some people believe she does not exist. Imagine someone who becomes more mysterious the more you know about her. Imagine Emily Dickinson.

In fact Emily Dickinson was very real, leaving a legacy of almost 1,800 poems and many letters. And though at a certain point in her life she rarely left home—in 1865 Dickinson withdrew from society, stopped going to church, stopped going uptown, and stopped seeing most, but not all visitors to her home—Dickinson had an active mind and a style so unique that she is considered one of America's great poets. Yet it is that same originality that makes her difficult to know.

A December Day, 1830

It was a very cold December day in Amherst, Massachusetts, a Friday. Emily Norcross Dickinson was going to have her second child. She was probably a bit nervous. Her mother and sister could not come from their home in Monson (a town little more than fifteen miles from Amherst) and she was not on very good terms with her husband's mother or sisters. She had no close women friends in or around Amherst. Because of her status as Edward Dickinson's wife, she would not use a midwife, who might offer emotional support and let nature run its course. Rather, her new baby was to be delivered by Dr. Isaac Cutler, an experienced doctor who had brought her first child, William Austin, into the world.

Still, Dr. Cutler's specialty was not delivering babies, and most men who practiced medicine (for by and large, men were doctors then) viewed pregnancy as a form of sickness. Emily Norcross knew that women often died in childbirth and that in her family in particular there were rumors about sickly infants.[1] Then there was Mr Stebbins. He was painting

Mrs. Dickinson's bedroom that very day. Emily Norcross had wanted to have it done earlier, but her husband would not allow it. Nevertheless, she had secretly asked the paper hanger to come, and he was just finishing.[2] It was into this household that Emily Elizabeth Dickinson was born on December 10, 1830, at 5:00 in the morning.

AMHERST AND AMERICA, 1830

Of course, the world was very different in 1830. Railroads were beginning to crisscross the country, connecting places that were formerly unreachable. People thought of train travel the way we think of travel to other planets. Canals, like the Erie Canal, had been completed, thus providing water routes from the East Coast to the middle of the country. What this did for the economy and the lives of people is astounding. Goods from the South, such as cotton, could be shipped to the North. And people in Amherst and the Northeast were gradually able to connect with people elsewhere in the developing nation. Still, in 1830, Amherst was fairly agrarian, meaning that most people were farmers and the economy was based on agriculture.

Emily, however, was born into a family of scholars

and lawyers. Her grandfather, Samuel Fowler Dickinson, founded Amherst College, which still exists today. Samuel Dickinson was known to be pious, or religious, and a hard and steady worker. Because of the Puritan heritage of the northeastern part of this country, such values were highly regarded. So, although the Dickinson family was not wealthy, they were well-known.

LIFE AT THE DICKINSONS'S

When Emily was born, the family lived on Main Street in a large brick house called the Homestead. It was said to be the first brick house in Amherst. Three years later, her sister Lavinia was born, completing the family. There were always dogs, and Emily was fond of one in particular, Carlo. When Emily was nine, the family moved around the corner to North Pleasant Street.

When Emily was growing up, children were supposed to be seen and not heard. At a very early age, girls amused themselves quietly indoors with their dolls and sewing. Most of the books children read were printed in England during the 1700s and then reprinted here in America over and over. Usually, these books had themes from the Bible or were stories about the importance of being hardworking, honest, and obedient. Probably Emily learned to read from just such books. There were also a few fairy tales she would have known, many of which are still told today, such as "Hansel and Gretel," "Rapunzel," and "Cinderella."

Before Emily was born, only certain sports were acceptable and then only for boys, who played after school and on weekends. These included activities such as hunting, fishing, boating, and swimming. By 1830, educators were considering the merits of sports for providing moral guidance. Parents starting sending their children to private instructors after school to learn "refined" sports, such as light gymnastics and marching as a class. By about 1860, many sports were advocated as healthy, useful, and pleasurable physical activities for young boys. The need for physical activity for girls was also suggested, but sports for girls were not strongly advocated by educators of the day.

Death was more commonplace in those days. A simple sore throat might have lethal consequences, and many a Sunday sermon dealt with mortality and resurrection. And in the new Dickinson house, Death was also a neighbor since the village cemetery ran along one side of it. From a north facing window, Emily could watch funeral processions enter the

Emily Dickinson would spend nearly all of her
adult life in the Homestead, above.

cemetery's main gate. Some scholars speculate that Dickinson's fascination in writing about loss and fatality may have stemmed from the years she spent living on Pleasant Street. Twelve years later, the family moved back to their original home on Main Street, and it was there Emily lived for the rest of her life.

Even though times were very different, kids back then felt about their parents as many do today. In a letter to a friend, Emily's brother Austin wrote that father and mother had gone away for an overnight trip: "Emily and I are left lord and lady of the mansion with none to molest or make us afraid. We are anticipating a fine time in the absence of the ancient people. Wish you were here to help make us laugh."[3]

The family remained close, and when Austin married Susan Gilbert in 1856, Emily was overjoyed (Susan and Emily had met at school). Emily's father built a home for the couple next to his own, called The Evergreens.

EDUCATING EMILY

Considering that most people viewed education for women and especially adolescent girls as unnecessary, sending Emily to school was a very progressive move. But Edward Dickinson's chief concern for all three of his children (in addition to their health and their duty to be pleasant and obedient) was their education. In this, he echoed his own father's life-long dedication and the atmosphere of the town in which he and his family lived. Even before the college was founded, Amherst had a large number of scholars, such as Noah Webster (famous compiler of the first printed dictionary of "American" English in 1828) and Lucius Boltwood, another of Amherst College's founding fathers and brother-in-law to Ralph Waldo Emerson, the famous idealist poet.

The first school that Edward urged all his children to attend was a two-story building of whitewashed brick on the same street as their house. Next, Emily attended Amherst Academy down the street. Classes were as academically demanding as some colleges are today, but Emily was an outstanding student. "We have a very fine school," she wrote proudly to her friend Abiah Root. "There are Mental Philosophy, Geology, Latin, and Botany. How large they sound, don't they?"[4] In many ways, she was a typical teenager. She liked some teachers better than others and gossiped about who was dating whom.

In September 1847, Emily entered the Mount Holyoke Female Seminary in South Hadley, Massachusetts, ten miles south of Amherst. The Seminary founded by Mary Lyon in 1837 was innovative for its approach to women's education: there

A portrait of a young Emily Dickinson.

were rigorous academic entrance requirements, a demanding curriculum, and, conspicuously, no classes in homemaking, though each student had domestic duties. These girls were to be real scholars.

But the school was also quite strict. Every fifteen minutes, bells rang to announce the next activity. The students were expected to obey some seventy rules regarding conduct, health, protection of the building, safety, and contact with the outside world. For example, they had to whisper in halls and work rooms, sleep with doors slightly open, and sit in assigned seats at every activity. Miss Lyon believed strongly in religion, and students were required to attend church services, chapel talks, prayer meetings, and Bible study groups. Twice a day teachers and students spent time in private devotions.

Though she was excited by the prospect of the new school, it took Emily a while to get used to being away, as can be seen in this letter to her brother:

> South Hadley, 21 October 1847
>
> My dear Brother. Austin. I can't tell you now how much good your visit did me. My cough is almost gone & my spirits have wonderfully lightened since then. I had a great mind to be homesick after you went home, but I concluded not to, & therefore gave up all homesick feelings. Was not that a wise determination? How have you all been at home since last week? I suppose nothing of serious

importance has occurred, or I should have heard of it, before this time. I received a loving letter from Mary Warner, last evening & if you see her, please give my love to her & tell her I will answer it the first moment, I have to spare from school.[5]

And then there was the question of religious faith. In the time in which Emily grew up, religious revivals were common in New England. Amherst and surrounding towns clung to Puritan beliefs even as other towns such as Boston began to experience great

MOUNT HOLYOKE

Mount Holyoke College exists today and is still an all-women's college, though probably you won't find students whispering in the halls. About 2,200 students from all over the United States and 80 countries around the world attend the college. It was the first school in the cluster of women's colleges known as the "Seven Sisters," a name that comes from the Pleiades star cluster (a constellation containing seven stars). The distinguished colleges that make up the academic constellation are:

Barnard, Bryn Mawr, Radcliffe, Smith, Vassar, Wellesley, and, of course, Mount Holyoke.

The "Seven Sisters" nickname was adopted in 1927, when the schools organized to promote private, independent women's colleges and "separate but equal" liberal arts education for women. Until that time, most colleges and universities were open to men only.

social changes and radically new and different ways of thinking about God and society. Perhaps because Edward Dickinson traveled back and forth between villages and large metropolitan areas, and the family read several newspapers and all the best journals, Emily may have been exposed to some of these ideas. It was hard for her to accept the religious underpinnings of Mount Holyoke. Writing to Abiah about another friend, she gives us a glimmer of her doubt:

> I presume you have heard from Abby, and know what she now believes—she makes a sweet, girl Christian, religion makes her face quite different, calmer, but full of radiance, holy, yet very joyful. She talks of herself quite freely, seems to love Lord Christ most dearly, and to wonder, and be bewildered, at the life she has always led. It all looks black, and distant, and God, and Heaven are near, she is certainly very much changed.
>
> She has told you about things here, how the "still small voice" is calling, and how the people are listening, and believing, and truly obeying— how the place is very solemn, and sacred, and the bad ones slink away, and are sorrowful—not at their wicked lives—but at this strange time, great change. I am one of the lingering bad ones, and so do I slink away, and pause, and ponder, and ponder, and pause, and do work without knowing why— not surely for this brief world, and more sure it is not for Heaven—and I ask what this message means that they ask for so very eagerly, you know

of this depth, and fulness, will you try to tell me about it?[6]

In spite of the fact that Edward Dickinson believed in educating his daughters, he was not without biases. He did not think much of most of the popular writers of the day such as Harriet Beecher Stowe and Emerson. His ideas were rooted in nineteenth century Puritan New England; he believed in moderation, hard work, the power of reason over passion, and the virtue of self-denial. Novels, he thought, were frivolous. In an 1862 letter, Dickinson wrote of her father:

> I have a Brother and Sister—My Mother does not care for thought—and Father, too busy with his Briefs—to notice what we do—He buys me many Books—but begs me not to read them—because he fears they joggle the mind.[7]

And what few professional women there were, Edward did not hold in high regard. While engaged to Emily's mother, Mr. Dickinson wrote a series of articles for an Amherst newspaper under the pseudonym of "Coelebs." He claimed that women, while they should be educated, had their duties to perform—namely: childrearing, cooking, and cleaning. Imagine the problem for Emily, challenging her father's conventional and religious viewpoints. Her questioning nature would contribute to the strength of her poetry.

Eventually Emily came home without finishing Mount Holyoke. There were probably a number of reasons for this, such as poor health and her rebellion against the religiousness and strictness of the seminary. Her father may have wanted her home, or perhaps she never got used to being away.

HOUSEWORK

Do you hate to do certain chores around your house? Well, Emily did too. In nineteenth-century America housework was very hard and people hired servants (or *domestics*) to undertake these chores. Since matches had not been invented, servants maintained the fires used for heating and cooking. Just to keep a house running, servants had to cut and haul wood, sweep and haul ashes, and clean up the soot when poorly vented chimneys smoked in a downdraft. There were candles to make or smoky lamps to fill and trim.

Kitchen chores included open-fire cooking and maneuvering iron cranes, spits, and heavy cast-iron pots. Utensils turned black with soot. To gauge the temperature of an oven, the cook had to hold her hand inside the heated oven and count the number of seconds she could tolerate the pain. Just think how hot the kitchen would be in summer! Until refrigeration was introduced in about 1834, meat spoiled in a day, and poultry could not be killed more than four hours before it was cooked. Milk soured in half that time. Water was hand-carried, often from inside the house to a washing house outside, so doing laundry was a long and tiring task.

Emily's mother spent time cooking and caring for sick relatives and friends in addition to managing her own busy household. Even with the help of Emily and Lavinia and a woman named Mrs. Mack hired to help with the laundry, Mrs. Dickinson still had a lot of housework.

Following their mother's lead, the Dickinson sisters baked for neighbors and, in their own home, developed the habit of splitting the work during periods when they did not have additional help or their mother was ill. Cleaning fell most often to Lavinia, while Emily was cook and baker. Dickinson once wrote, "I dont keep the Moth part of the House—I keep the Butterfly part."[8]

On top of it all, remember that the Dickinsons were a prominent family in town, very involved with its society. As part of Amherst College, Edward Dickinson and his wife were well known for their commencement receptions. There was a "steady stream of visitors, many of them famous or near-famous, who enjoyed their hospitality."[9]

Not only was Edward Dickinson the treasurer of

Amherst College for thirty-seven years, he was also a lifelong trustee of Amherst Academy and very involved in local affairs such as the town meeting and the First Church Parish Committee.

Throughout her life, Dickinson wrote about the housework she did. Sometimes she complained that her parents "regulated" and "settled" her and her sister Vinnie with housework (letter 182). In the 1840s she describes herself as doing "everything," mentioning the piles of mending that awaited her return after a month away with relatives (letters 5, 9, 14). In the early 1850s, many of the poet's letters to friends addressed how hard she had to work. She complained to friend Jane Humphrey in 1850, "Vinnie away—and my two hands but two—not four, or five as they ought to be—and so many wants— and me so very handy—and my time of so little account—and my writing so very needless" (letter 30). Eventually Dickinson's father placed an ad for a maid.

PEOPLE IN EMILY'S LIFE

WANTED: Competent girl to do general household chores. Must be clean and reliable. Apply at Brick House on Main Street between the hours of noon and 2 pm.

—Typical ad appearing in the *Springfield Daily News*

In 1869, the Dickinsons hired Maggie Maher, an Irish immigrant, to be their maid. Before long, however, she would become much more than a maid or a cook to the family. Says one Dickinson scholar, "Emily and Maggie formed a relationship that was at once unfair and close."[10] It was Maggie who undertook a lot of the extra housework so that Emily could write. Many Dickinson scholars also believe that Maggie knew about Emily's writing and later protected at least some of it from being burned.

CLASS DISTINCTIONS

The Dickinsons were part of the middle class, well-off enough to hire domestics to work in their houses and gardens. Many of the people hired to do household jobs were Irish immigrants who were not always well-treated and often were not seen as equals. In fact, "behavior" books for young upper- and middle-class women included instructions about how to treat servants. These behavior books also stressed the need to create segregation between the classes. Emily and her sister Lavinia would have been familiar with them.

But by all accounts, Emily did not entirely pay attention to those behavior books. For example, she chose Tom Kelley (Maggie's brother) as her chief pallbearer, along with five other Irish men who worked the Homestead grounds. For Irish Catholics, the significance of this honor would not go unnoticed, nor would Dickinson be unaware of it.

Josiah Holland

MY SAFEST FRIENDS: THE PEOPLE DICKINSON KNEW

Emily is almost thirty and has just met a remarkable man at Austin and Sue's. He is rather handsome and has a wonderful personality. He is funny and smart. As editor of his father's paper, the *Springfield Daily Republican*, he writes clear and pointed editorials. In fact, he is well on his way to making the paper nationally respected. His name is Samuel Bowles, and he is known for his independent thinking. He is also a bit of a ladies' man, a bit self-absorbed. But Emily does not care about that as much as finding someone to parry with her. So she sits down to write him, beginning a correspondence that will last almost twenty years.

EMILY'S FRIENDS

> My friends are my "estate." Forgive me then the avarice to hoard them! They tell me those were poor early, have different views of gold. I dont know how that is. God is not so wary as we, else he would give us no friends, lest we forget him![11]

Who else did Emily Dickinson choose for friends? Josiah Holland, also an editor at the *Daily Republican*, for one. Emily knew him and his wife Elizabeth, and they too came to call at The Evergreens. Only a few

A rear view of the Evergreens, which was built for Austin and Sue by Edward Dickinson.

years older than Emily, Elizabeth became a favorite of the poet and her sister Lavinia. They visited the Hollands in Springfield and throughout the poet's life Mrs. Holland remained Emily's closest female friend outside the family.

While at Amherst Academy, Emily had been a very lively and sociable companion. She made many friends, but the two girls she corresponded with most were Abiah Root and Jane Humphrey. Though she wrote them many letters, they do not appear to have captivated her as they got older, and eventually those correspondences stopped.

At Amherst Academy, Emily also met Susan Gilbert, and they became quite close by 1850. When Susan married Emily's brother Austin in 1856, Emily wrote her a little poem in about 1858 with this first stanza:

One Sister I have in our house
And one, a hedge away.
There's only one recorded,
But both belong to me.[12]

Susie was an important person to Emily and probably knew her poetry well. But as time went on, relations between the two became strained. Emily may have felt left out during the early years of Sue's and Austin's marriage, and later when he had an affair with Mabel Loomis Todd and Emily (devoted as always to her brother) sided with him.

Another of Dickinson's early associations was with Benjamin Franklin Newton of Worcester, Massachusetts. He was a law student in Mr. Dickinson's office late in 1847, and though it is reported he did not attend college, he must have had an intellect and seriousness that Emily's father respected. The men in Edward's office were always welcome at the Dickinson home, so Mr. Newton visited there. He introduced the Dickinson girls to the writing of the Brontës and Emerson and is probably one of the few of Emily's earliest friends who was able to recognize her promise as a poet.

Emily may have been possessive about her friendships, and she also seems to have associated friendships with fear and loss. In 1853, Ben Newton died. A few days after he died she wrote a note to her brother: "Oh Austin, Newton is dead. The first of my own friends."[13] He was still on her mind twenty years later when she wrote another correspondent, "My dying Tutor told me that he would like to live till I had been a poet."[14]

There is also evidence that she loved a man named Otis Phillips Lord. A graduate of Amherst College, Lord studied law and was admitted to the bar in 1835. Emily was twenty-six when she met him, and he was married. They wrote each other often, and when Mrs. Lord died in 1877, they began to enjoy what Emily's niece called "adventures in conversation."[15] Most of all, he was fun, literate and intellectual; in short, he understood Ms. Dickinson.

There are two later, important friendships for Dickinson. One with Colonel Thomas Wentworth Higginson, a radical minister of the Free Church in Worcester, Massachusetts. The other with Charles Wadsworth, a Presbyterian pastor Dickinson is thought to have met while visiting a friend in Philadelphia.

With Higginson, the poet maintained a friendship from the 1860s until her death. As people did in those days before cell phones and email, the two wrote letters. Dickinson initiated the correspondence in 1862 when Higginson was a published writer and critic. Most Dickinson scholars think that Emily saw the lead article Higginson had written for a famous literary magazine called *The Atlantic Monthly*. The article, titled "Letter to a Young Contributor," gave practical advice to beginning writers and made a call for submissions. Many Dickinson experts agree that Emily must have read the article and felt encouraged to write him. Whatever compelled her, their correspondence lasted twenty-one years, and though it is said that Higginson did not really understand her verse or publish it during her lifetime, she did choose him to be her critic and often sought his advice on her work. He, for his part, considered Emily's poetry difficult, but he also appeared to think she was worthy of his time and attention.

Helen Hunt Jackson, a poet and novelist who had grown up in Amherst, was one writer who had confidence in Dickinson. The two had lost contact over the years, and Colonel Higginson re-acquainted them. Mabel Loomis Todd also believed in Dickinson's originality and talent. Though she never actually met Dickinson, she later collaborated with

Helen Hunt Jackson

Higginson to produce the first published collection of the poet's work.

CHANGING AMHERST

As Dickinson grew, so did the factories in Amherst. Two of the largest made hats—the Leonard Hills Company and the Henry D. Ferring Company. The Dickinsons could see both factories from their windows. All in all, life was good. The Dickinsons were for the most part a well thought-of, even influential, family.

But trouble was brewing. Because the country's economy was expanding so rapidly, some people wanted the government to provide protective tariffs (taxes) on imports.

People in the North and the growing western part of the country wanted the federal government to sponsor the building of roads, railroads, and canals. The South, however, had little interest in these projects. As public lands in the West were beginning to be settled, the focus turned toward free farming. Quarrels developed over the high tariffs, which protected the Northern manufacturers. The South wanted a low tariff so it could trade its cotton to Great Britain and other countries for cheap foreign goods. Thus began the Civil War.

Though Amherst was never directly in the line of

fire, it was affected. By the time the war was over, the town had lost most of its quaint New England ways, and more and more people were moving from the country into the larger cities, seeking better prospects than farm life could offer. At the same time, immigrants from Europe poured into metropolitan areas all over the country, and despite the enormous causalities on both sides during the Civil War, America's population increased to over 38 million. Then over 11 million additional immigrants arrived and the nation was transformed forever.

Even though Emily Dickinson is often described as reclusive or withdrawn, she was not oblivious to the events going on around her. She read newspapers and journals and would have been aware of all the changes going on in the world. Still, she withdrew and devoted herself to her craft: the art of writing.

THIS IS MY LETTER TO THE WORLD

This is my letter to the world,
That never wrote to me,—
The simple news that Nature told,
With tender majesty.

Her message is committed
To hands I cannot see;

For love of her, sweet countrymen,
Judge tenderly of me!

Emily Dickinson broke ground with her unusual use of language and punctuation, the breadth of her subject matter, and her reclusive, unconventional lifestyle. Whether seen as the Belle or Myth of Amherst, today nearly all her writings are recognized as American classics. In truth, Emily Dickinson was quite a Somebody.

HOW TO READ A POEM

Understanding the Poetry
of Emily Dickinson

There is more to poetry than just the words themselves. What William Shakespeare called "the mind's eye" also plays a role.[1] What that means is that *your* experiences and thoughts will add to your understanding. Poems, unlike novels or newspapers, require a bit more attention to detail. Read them slowly and carefully, and try reading them aloud.

When you first approach a poem, some things may make sense to you immediately. For example, the following poem Dickinson wrote in about 1868, when she was almost forty years old.

Tell all the Truth but tell it slant—
Success in Circuit lies
Too bright for our infirm Delight
The Truth's superb surprise

As Lightning to the Children eased
With explanation kind
The Truth must dazzle gradually
Or every man be blind—

In this poem, consider the word "circuit." It comes from the word "circle" and can mean an indirect route. One interpretation is that the way to the truth may not be the most direct route ("Tell all the Truth but tell it slant/Success in Circuit lies").

By capitalizing the words "Truth" and "Circuit," Dickinson employs a commonly used poetic device, *personification*; that is, she makes "Truth" and "Circuit" proper nouns, like people.

DICKINSON'S LITERARY DEVICES AND CONVENTIONS

Like many poets, Dickinson used an assortment of literary devices: *metaphor* (comparing two objects with the intent of giving clearer meaning to one of them, usually with forms of the verb "to be" such as "is" or "was"), *simile* (comparing two objects using a specific word of comparison such as "like," "as," or "than"), *alliteration* (the repetition of sounds) and *symbolism* (a form of metaphor in which a person, place, thing, or quality takes on a more complex meaning).

PUNCTUATION

Unlike many writers of her time, Dickinson did not use conventional rhyme, capitalization, or punctuation. For example, she put dashes not just at the end of a line, but also within the lines.

Examine this poem:

The Brain—is wider than the Sky—
For—put them side by side—
The one the other will contain
With ease—and You—beside—.

Notice that lines two and four contain interior dashes that help control the poem's rhythm. Emily Dickinson is widely believed to be the first well-known poet to use dashes this way. Some believe she used the dash for emphasis, to indicate a missing word or words, or to replace a comma or period. Other readers suggest that the dashes are similar to the punctuation and meter of the sort of hymnal with which Dickinson would have been familiar.

CAPITALIZATION

Another feature of Dickinson's poetry is unusual capitalization. How many times have you been corrected for not properly punctuating a sentence? Have you been reminded that only proper nouns—that is, the names of persons, places, or things—are capitalized?

In many of her poems Dickinson capitalizes common as well as proper nouns.[2] Though she may have derived her use of capitals from German, which she studied at the Amherst Academy, such usage has other effects, one of which is making common things seem more important.

For example, a "spider" becomes a "Spider," as if it possessed a proper name and a personality. In addition, the unusual use of capitalization is eye-catching.

Though in the early twentieth century most poetry was written to be heard, that notion of verse was beginning to change. Starting perhaps as early as Dickinson, the focus began to shift to a poem's visual properties. Some critics think that Dickinson may have even moved that process along by rebelling against the conventions of grammar and punctuation.[3]

METER AND RHYME

Dickinson used meter, the rhythmical pattern of syllables stressed in lines of verse, in a way not found in most nineteenth century poetry. Many of her poems consist of alternating lines of eight and six syllables, known as *common meter*. Back then such a scheme was used in American nursery rhymes and in hymns.

She also experimented with traditional rhyme schemes, frequently replacing them with partial rhymes or with words that sounded alike but did not quite rhyme. Sometimes she used sight rhymes, sometimes in the form of visual jokes such as words that are spelled as if they rhyme but do not (for example, *word* and *lord*).

Sometimes, Dickinson used no rhymes at all, and while that may not seem so unusual today, it was extraordinary at the time.

OTHER VISUAL ASPECTS OF DICKINSON'S POETRY

One may wonder about the layout of Dickinson's poems on a page and how she decided where to break lines. "Your thoughts dont have words every day" she says in one of her poems (#1452), and perhaps this line echoes your own feelings about trying to write. In addressing the challenge of finding just the right word for a thought, Dickinson puzzled over the many ways to place words on the page. We know because she left behind a copy of this poem with a dozen different words and phrases crossed out and placed differently within the poem. It's also important to realize that Dickinson used letter-writing as her vehicle, sometimes intermingling letter and poem. And although she was not the only person to do this (her Aunt Elizabeth once sent Austin a rhymed letter of fifty stanzas about his toothache), she was quite inventive and prolific.

LANGUAGE/DICTION

As for all writers, words were Dickinson's tools. But the way she used the words was unusual. While other women authors wrote in a long, flowery style, Emily Dickinson fit her complex ideas into short, tight sentences with a vocabulary that most women did not use. Dickinson critic Charles Anderson comments that Emily Dickinson "In her best writing was never at the mercy of her emotions."[4] Rather, "she mastered her themes by controlling her language."[5] She borrowed the words of many professions, such as law, medicine, and the military, and she took her meter from English hymns. Small wonder that composers like Aaron Copeland have set her poems to music and dancers like Martha Graham wanted to choreograph them.

Dickinson loved language and enjoyed words for their own sake. One of her amusements was reading Webster's Dictionary (1844), savoring words and their definitions. A number of her poems take as their form definitions of words—for example, "Success Is Counted Sweetest," "The Bible is an Antique Volume," and "Hope is the Thing with Feathers."

FASCICLES

Emily Dickinson collected her poems in *fascicles*. She drafted the poems on whatever paper was at hand (even the backs of envelopes), then copied them onto pieces of folded, unlined paper, often striking out words and adding others. She arranged the sheets of paper in a stack, punched two holes on the left side, and bound them together with string, creating packets of sixteen pages containing twenty or more poems. In 1981, Ralph Franklin compiled *The Manuscript Books of Emily Dickinson*, arranging the poems as close to the way Dickinson arranged them as possible. This collection of the fascicles lets us see the poet's unconventional use of punctuation as well as her deliberation over different words. Not surprisingly, the existence of the overlapping versions has made for many interpretations of Dickinson's poetry.

When Dickinson died in 1860, 1,775 poems were found bound into fascicles.

Maggie Maher, the Irish maid who worked for the Dickinsons for over twenty years, did a lot to protect the fascicles. Apparently Emily stored many of them in Maggie's trunk. As was common practice in the 1800s, Dickinson asked that her correspondence be burned after she died.[6] Since many of her poems were contained in letters, when Lavinia burned them, she burned the poems as well. But according to Dickinson's niece, Martha Dickinson Bianchi, Maggie came to Sue and Austin with the writings stored in her trunk "in an act of disobedience that preserved a literary treasure."[7]

FASCICLES *(continued)*

Maggie was also the person responsible for handing over her copy of a daguerreotype you often see reproduced in books on Emily Dickinson. Taken in about 1847 when Emily was seventeen years old, it is the only uncontested photo we have of her today.

In April 2000, Philip F. Gura , a professor of American literature at the University of North Carolina, placed a bid on eBay for a "vintage Emily Dickinson albumen photo." (*Albumen*, the white of an egg, was used in a common process for developing photographs in the mid-1860s.) Professor Gura won the bid and went about trying to authenticate the picture. It is an exciting story, but not everyone is convinced the photo is authentic. Writes Gura, "I (and many others) continue to believe that the image genuinely is of Dickinson, and my state of mind regarding it was beautifully summed up in an editorial about the image in the (Durham) Herald-Sun. . . . Although the forensic analysis of Gura's photo strongly suggests the woman is ED, no one can say for sure. By the same token, no one apparently can say that the woman is NOT Dickinson. Thus is Philip Gura caught in neutral buoyancy between belief and hope. Or, maybe that's the way ED wanted.'"[8]

Dickinson changed the function or part of speech of a word, using adjectives and verbs as nouns. For example, in "We Talk in Careless—and in Loss," "careless" is an adjective used as a noun. She frequently uses "be" instead of "is" or "are."

Her linguistic mastery and sense of the dramatic combine as she creates striking first lines for her poems, such as "The Brain is Wider than the Sky," "I Felt a Funeral in My Brain," and "A Route of Evanescence."

Occasionally, it seems as though Dickinson created private meanings and symbols, using them as if everyone else was in on their meaning. So there are times when her language, instead of communicating, can be baffling. Consulting a nineteenth-century dictionary may also be useful in grasping Dickinson's meaning, at times.

CHARACTER TYPES

In many poems, Dickinson does not identify a particular character. However, this does not mean that a poem does not have one. For example, in "I'm Nobody! Who are you?" the speaker asserts that being a "nobody" is a much better lifestyle than being judged or even observed by an "admiring bog." In this instance, the bog is like a character.

The only verifiable photograph of Emily Dickinson (above).

I'm Nobody! Who are you?
Are you—Nobody—too?
Then there's a pair of us!
Don't tell! they'd advertise—you know!

How dreary—to be—Somebody!
How public—like a Frog—
To tell one's name—the livelong June—
To an admiring Bog!

Dickinson's biographers often mention that she preferred a life of seclusion to a life of admiration. Could the "nobody" to whom Dickinson refers be the person she longed to be?

COMMON THEMES IN EMILY DICKINSON'S POETRY

Dickinson's writing deals with all the stuff of life: nature, love and death, time and eternity. She treated these themes in a manner all her own: often with humor and playfulness, but also with seriousness and sensitivity. Many of her poems use the pronoun "I" as their central speaker or *persona*. This "I" seems to speak directly to us, making observations that are at once obvious and indecipherable. As writer Joyce Carol Oates once suggested, what Emily Dickinson questions is "meaning itself."[9]

Dickinson took her writing very seriously and

The cover to the 1896 edition of Emily Dickinson's
Poems, edited by Mabel Loomis Todd.

dedicated herself to finding poetry in every aspect of day-to-day life. The themes of life: love, spirituality, or the belief in something outside the physical world, and jealousy and despair, repeat themselves throughout her work.

Though Dickinson's insights are profound, some think they are limited in topic. The critic Northrop Frye once commented that he would be hard pressed

DOES THE SOUND FIT THE SENSE?

One measure of good poetry is to ask yourself "Does the sound fit the sense?" Poets write with an ear to the "music" of their words. They use various sound devices to make their verses "sing" so that their work has an enhanced meaning when read aloud. The music in poetry is not always pretty; a poem about a horse may have a short, clipped sound, while a poem about the incoming tide may have a pounding, urgent rhythm.

Before the twentieth century, poetry was generally characterized by certain formal sound and structure devices such as meter. Meter is the pattern of beats and pauses that creates the rhythm of poetic verse. In Emily Dickinson's time, if it did not have meter, it was not poetry. Modern poets have written increasingly in *free verse*, poetry without a set rhyme scheme or meter. Still, poets writing free verse use many sound devices and may create their music by using *alliteration*, *assonance*, and *onomatopoeia*. Emily Dickinson uses all of these to create a unique voice and to enhance meaning in her poems.

Emily Dickinson's writing desk, as it appears reproduced today a the Homestead.

to name another English-speaking poet with so little interest in social or political events. And though Dickinson lived through the Civil War, until recently scholars thought she wrote little about it. As you will see, the war did surface in Dickinson's poetry, but its presence is not overt.

APPROACHING EMILY DICKINSON

"Dickinson's poetry is challenging because it is radical and original in its rejection of most traditional nineteenth-century themes and techniques."[10] Read her poems actively, paying attention with all your senses. It may even help to read them aloud; what may seem puzzling on "a silent page"[11] can make more sense if you hear it, listening for the pauses around the dashes, the sounds of the words themselves.

If you think Emily Dickinson leaves a lot out of her writing, you are not alone. But look carefully. Dickinson used a wide range of poetic devices, as well as some fairly unusual syntax and grammar. Because her use of dashes is sometimes puzzling, try reading her poems aloud to hear how carefully the words are arranged. What may seem intimidating on a silent page can surprise you when you actually hear it. Also

Emily Dickinson's bedroom at the Homestead in Amherst.

keep in mind that Dickinson, like every human being, was not always consistent in her views; her viewpoint can change from poem to poem. It seems she was less interested in finding answers to questions than in examining their meaning, their "circumference."

INTERPRETATION

"There have been, there are now, and there will continue to be contests over not only who owns Emily Dickinson's words but what object can be called a

49

ARRANGING THE POEMS

Dickinson was a prolific writer who left behind many, many poems. They were in quite a state: some had been hastily stuffed into Maggie Maher's trunk, Lavinia had burned some, and Dickinson had bound others together with needle and thread into the fascicles. In 1955, a three-volume critical edition edited by Thomas H. Johnson set a new standard for Emily Dickinson students and scholars the world over. His book contained 1,775 poems in chronological order (as far as he could determine). He examined the originals and published them in their first form, leaving out other editors' punctuation marks and titles.

In 1967, another Dickinson scholar, Ralph W. Franklin, revised Johnson's ordering and added some other poems he had found. Mr. Franklin kept working on this project until 1981, when he attempted to fully restore the poet's original arrangement. Guided by such evidence as the imperfections of her stationery, smudge patterns, and puncture marks where Dickinson's needle had pierced the paper to bind them, Franklin returned the poems to their original order. Still more recently, Sharon Cameron argued that the way Emily Dickinson bound her poems had less to do with the order in which she wrote them (the chronology) than with their theme. [12]

poem by Emily Dickinson. There are many objects that can be called poems of Emily Dickinson, but what constitutes a poem by her has never been firmly established."[13]

Only ten of what most would call Dickinson's poems were published during her lifetime and then only anonymously. Because her style was so unusual and experimental, her original editors (Thomas Wentworth Higginson and Mabel Loomis Todd) tried to conceal it. They thought her peculiar punctuation was an obstacle to reading rather than an integral aspect of her verse, so they "corrected" it, along with her spelling, many of her rhymes, and other unusual features of her poems in manuscript. For this reason, her work appears in different ways, sometimes with inline dashes, sometimes without. In one version a word may appear with initial capitals while in another collection the word will be in lower case.

In addition, Dickinson never gave any of her poems titles; Todd and Higginson did. Todd and Higginson also grouped the poems according to principles of their own that did not reflect Dickinson's arrangement. These groupings included:

- Time and Eternity
- Life/Love
- Nature

In the following chapters, we will look at

Mabel Loomis Todd

Dickinson's better-known works and try to unravel their meaning in a process called *explication*, which literally means "an unfolding." We will refer to the poems and letters by the number that Thomas H. Johnson, one of the first scholars to organize her work, gave them.

FOR FURTHER STUDY

Several Dickinson poems mentioned earlier are worthy of further study. Note the word choices and use of language and see if you can find any additional significance in any of these poems.

Success is counted sweetest
By those who ne'er succeed.
To comprehend a nectar
Requires sorest need.

Not one of all the purple host
Who took the flag to-day
Can tell the definition,
So clear, of victory,

As he, defeated, dying,
On whose forbidden ear
The distant strains of triumph
Break, agonized and clear.

***

Hope is the thing with feathers
That perches in the soul,

And sings the tune without the words,
And never stops at all,

And sweetest in the gale is heard;
And sore must be the storm
That could abash the little bird
That kept so many warm.

I've heard it in the chillest land,
And on the strangest sea;
Yet, never, in extremity,
It asked a crumb of me.

***

The Bible is an antique volume
Written by faded men,
At the suggestion of Holy Spectres—
Subjects—Bethlehem—
Eden—the ancient Homestead—
Satan—the Brigadier,
Judas—the great Defaulter,
David—the Troubadour.
Sin—a distinguished Precipice
Others must resist,
Boys that "believe"
Are very lonesome—
Other boys are "lost."
Had but the tale a warbling Teller
All the boys would come—
Orpheus' sermon captivated,
It did not condemn.

I Heard a Fly Buzz

Death and Eternity in Dickinson

Emily Dickinson spent much of her early life in a house whose windows looked out on a cemetery. More than that, children knew that many illnesses could prove fatal. Diphtheria, scarlet fever, and whooping cough were common diseases in the 1800s, and many children died before they reached the age of sixteen from the sorts of things we do not even think about today: minor cuts and scratches that became infected or cures administered by well-meaning parents and doctors that were actually harmful. Death was common and, being the keen observer she was, Dickinson often wrote about it.

Death as a Theme

Before the age of technology and medicine, people were more resigned to death. Friends and family often crowded into the dying person's room waiting and watching, as if death were a movie or play.

Commonly, people brought gifts, and those who had led less than ideal lives were urged to repent. Those gathered would sing hymns, and finally the dying person might whisper that he or she felt God in the room. Of course, not every death was like this, but such a scene would have been familiar to Emily Dickinson and her family.

Consider the images in this poem:

I heard a Fly buzz—when I died—
The Stillness in the Room
Was like the Stillness in the Air—
Between the Heaves of Storm—

The Eyes around—had wrung them dry—
And Breaths were gathering firm
For that last Onset—when the King
Be witnessed—in the Room—

I willed my Keepsakes—Signed away
What portion of me be
Assignable—and then it was
There interposed a Fly—

With Blue—uncertain stumbling Buzz—
Between the light—and me—
And then the Windows failed—and then
I could not see to see—

Dickinson critic Caroline Rogue suggests that this poem begins with a standard nineteenth-century deathbed scene. From the beginning, Dickinson builds the scene: the stillness of the room, the family members whose "Eyes around— had wrung them dry." But, notes Rogue, at the crucial moment, when the sufferer is about to draw his last breath, "There interposed a fly." And what kind of a fly? A noisy one, a fly "with Blue—uncertain stumbling Buzz."[1]

WHAT DO YOU THINK?

Many of Emily Dickinson's poems use *symbols*, things that represent other things. For example, a traffic light contains three symbols—red to symbolize the command Stop, yellow for Caution, and green for Go. Can you identify the object or situation in "I Heard a Fly Buzz" that is really supposed to stand for something else?

Why is the fly there? Some critics like the poet John Ciardi have interpreted it as "the last kiss of the world."[2] Others think the fly represents the realities of a Victorian household; flies were as present in death as in life and Dickinson could be saying that death is as commonplace as a fly. And yet there is the odd line, "With Blue—uncertain stumbling Buzz." How can a sound be blue? Perhaps what Dickinson intends to describe is what she thinks it is like to die. Instead of the great hereafter, could it be that people just slip from consciousness? That they fail to "see to see?" Charles Anderson[3] and Besty Erkkila[4] propose that underneath such a supposition lies a tremendous break from the conventional attitudes of the time.

In Chapter 2 we talked about some common poetic tools or devices. Here's a poem in which Dickinson masterfully uses *personification*:

Because I could not stop for Death—
He kindly stopped for me—
The Carriage held but just Ourselves—
And Immortality.

We slowly drove—He knew no haste
And I had put away
My labor and my leisure too,
For His Civility—

We passed the School, where Children strove
At Recess—in the Ring—
We passed the Fields of Gazing Grain—
We passed the Setting Sun—

Or rather—He passed Us—
The Dews drew quivering and Chill—
For only Gossamer, my Gown—
My Tippet—only Tulle—

We paused before a House that seemed
A Swelling of the Ground—
The Roof was scarcely visible—
The Cornice—in the Ground—

Since then—'tis Centuries—and yet
Feels shorter than the Day
I first surmised the Horses' Heads
Were toward Eternity—

To begin, this poem presents us with some very

vivid images: the setting sun, a horse-drawn carriage, a graveyard ("a House that seemed/A Swelling of the Ground"). By capitalizing "death" and referring to it as "he", Dickinson begins to give the noun the characteristics of a person, perhaps even modeling this "Death" on someone she knew. Death rides in a carriage with "I," and it's a special ride, for the carriage holds just the two of them. The poem continues:

> We slowly drove—He knew no haste
> And I had put away
> My labor and my leisure too
> For His Civility

The "I" in this poem knows the trip is final. So the "I" and Death drive leisurely, completely at ease. Indeed, Death's graciousness in stopping at a time when "I" was too busy to stop for him is a mark of special politeness. The "I" willingly puts her work away. Again, because this is her last ride, she can give away her spare moments too.[5]

> We passed the School, where Children strove
> At Recess—in the Ring—
> We passed the Fields of Gazing Grain—
> We passed the Setting Sun—
>
> Or rather—He passed Us—

Conscious that the "I" is leaving the world, Dickinson resists the sentimental and simply presents the scene: the school children, the fields of grain, and the setting sun. Here, she illustrates all there is about life: youth, maturity and age, and the passage of time in the daily rising and setting of the sun. Children will play, the grain must be harvested, and the day will end, just as life eventually ends for all of us. "[A]bsorbed in the Ring" of childhood games, the players at life do not even stop to look up at the passing carriage of death."[6]

Invoking nature's indifference, Dickinson gives "a kind of cold vitality by transferring the stare of the dead traveler's eyes to the 'Gazing Grain.' " Dickinson transfers the sureness of death "to the living corn while the corpse itself passes by on its journey to immortality"[7]—a very clever way of talking about a complex subject, especially considering that this is a time when poetry is written in a specific style, almost like a formula, and certain topics are dealt with in certain ways.

Then we read about the setting sun (a traditional symbol of death), and it is as if we are in the funeral train, passing the village schoolhouse, the fields, finally arriving at the graveyard. As they pass the sun and near the grave, the poem's cadence (rhythmic flow) of sounds begins to slow. Dickinson describes dew that is "quivering and chill." Some critics think that Dickinson is trying to imagine what it must be like to be buried in the cold, dark ground.

Strikingly, Dickinson uses "For Only Goassamer, My Gown—My Tippet—only Tulle." A tippet is a cape or a shawl. It was also the long black scarf Anglican clergymen wore over their robes during prayer, and at one time the word was used to refer to a hangman's rope. Tulle is a type of stiff fabric used for veils and shrouds.

Again Anderson provides a helpful interpretation. He points out that this is not the description of "conventional burial clothes." Rather, it sound like a bridal gown "but of a very special sort." Could Death be like a proud father taking his daughter to the altar? If so, the house they pause before ("We paused before a House that seemed/A swelling of the Ground") must be a grave, distinguished by the fact that its roof is "scarcely visible." "The Cornice—in the Ground" must be the trim on the coffin already in the soil.

But the true ingenuity here is the poet's ability to look beyond the physical boundaries of the world. There is something else in the carriage and in the poem besides Death and the speaker, something that exists outside time and location. That something is "Immortality."

Compare the previous poem, written in 1862, with this one written in 1858:

I never lost as much but twice,
And that was in the sod.
Twice have I stood a beggar
Before the door of God!

Angels—twice descending
Reimbursed my store—
Burglar! Banker—Father!
I am poor once more! (#49)

Here, the exactness of the rhymes gives a sharp and final feeling. The first two lines tell us that Dickinson has lost not one, but two people she cares about. Like a beggar, she feels empty without them as she enters the church. Though she believes they are in heaven, she seems to be calling out to a God who can take many forms and is many things to many people ("Burglar! Banker—Father!"). Still, it's not enough to call out to God: she is feeling her loss, saddened by her friends' absence. Around this time she lost Ben Newton and another friend, Leonard Humphrey.

TIME AND ETERNITY

Closely related to Dickinson's poems about death are those dealing with time and eternity. There is no doubt that Emily was influenced by the religious traditions of the time. God was supposed to be everywhere and be all-knowing. Sometimes her poetry reflects a fear and even anger at this God. Yet there are times when she seems to embrace traditional religious imagery and faith. Many of her poems suggest limits about what a person can know, giving us the idea that she believed in something more powerful than a single human being. At the same time, Dickinson expresses admiration for nature and the human mind.

Here's an example:

Safe in their Alabaster Chambers—
Untouched by Morning
And untouched by Noon—
Sleep the meek members of the Resurrection—
Rafter of satin,
And Roof of stone.

Light laughs the breeze
In her Castle above them—
Babbles the Bee in a stolid Ear,
Pipe the Sweet Birds in ignorant cadence—
Ah, what sagacity perished here! (#216)

According to scholar Alfred Habbeger,[8] when Emily sent the poem next door to her sister-in-law and Susan did not like the second stanza, Dickinson drafted another:

Grand go the Years—in the Crescent—above them—
Worlds scoop their Arcs—
And Firmaments—row—
Diadems—drop and Doges—surrender
Soundless as dots on a Disc of snow

There is a push and pull in this poem, *"stasis* (or steady state) and motion."[9] Most critics acknowledge that on one level the poem is about religion. Good Christians ("Meek members of the Resurrection") are not so important in the scheme of things. No matter how fancy their tombs, there is no way they will live again.

In the first stanza, Dickinson confers a religious view of death, including the confident belief that there is an afterlife. Here, she copies the language of the Bible and of Protestant hymns, especially in the line "Sleep the meek members of the Resurrection." But in the next stanza she directs our attention to what is going on above ground: the light laughter of the breeze, birds chirping, the "sagacity [that] perished here!" *Sagacity* means "perceptiveness," and here we might even say, "aliveness." Looking at the cold white tombs that lock out the sun, can we really believe there is life after death?

To critic Bernhard Frank, there's far more to this poem. "Within ten lines we are introduced to at least seven levels of imagery: religious, sociopolitical, mercenary [concerned only with money], architectural/geometric, nomadic, sexual and musical."[10] He notes what other critics have noted, namely that Dickinson may be mocking the Bible ("Blessed are the meek for they shall inherit the earth," Matthew

5:5) and saying that yes, in fact, the earth is all the living get; that there is nothing more beyond. Like other readers, he also points out that the word "safe" can have more than one meaning. A safe can be a bank vault, which introduces the notion of things that are valuable. "Everything in the poem seems to say, You are what you own: the dead of stanza 1 are ostentatiously buried in alabaster, their coffins lined with satin, their gravestones in place."[11]

Another way of reading this poem is to understand it as the conflict between religion and science. Written between 1859 and 1861, the poem reflects a time when the Christian world was shaken by the conflict between religion and science. Up until then people had believed in life after death, but with the appearance of new ideas about science, including Charles Darwin's *On the Origin of Species* (published in 1859), people were beginning to question that belief.

David Porter, Professor of English at the University of Massachusetts, Amherst, directs our attention to the sound patterns of the poem. He says the push-pull tension in it comes from the rhyme scheme, "for in the opening stanza which describes the tomb where resurrection is as yet unachieved, the rhyme is only approximate."[12] He goes on to show that the second stanza rhymes perfectly and that this gives it a sense of finality.

WHO WAS CHARLES DARWIN?

You may have heard of Charles Darwin, the English natural-ist who challenged contemporary beliefs about the creation of life on earth. In his famous work, *On the Origin of Species*, he gave evidence that life was not created by some divine overseer and that it did not go on forever. Darwin's theory of natural selection suggested that no one species is supe-rior to another or is guaranteed persistence over time. Darwin also introduced the idea of randomness as the dri-ving force behind the variety of types in the natural world. In short, he believed that those that best adapted to the changing environment would survive.

His idea of evolution did more than contradict the Bible, it raised the idea that things in the world had a scientific explanation. As part of his theory, Darwin also proposed a method for doing scientific research. This was disturbing to nineteenth century society. Although some could reconcile the facts of evolution with their religious beliefs, many oth-ers had their faith shaken. Many could not accept debate over evolution, or the heartlessness of the eat-or-be-eaten scenario of the natural world. Emily Dickinson, however, appears to have questioned the existence of God endlessly, searching for new symbols to believe in. Poem #216 is an example of that mind set.

Bernhard Frank also notices the poet's use of capitals and consonants. "The opening s sound establishes the key note of the poem, taken up again in "Satin" and "Stone": It is the sound of silence."[13] That s disappears for a while, only to return in stanza 2, next to the "plosive dental" d in "Diadems," "drops," "Doges" (dukes) and "dots." Moving between ds and ss, Dickinson takes us from the vibrancy of life to the silence of death.

At first glance Poem #216 seems simple. Each stanza is self-contained and presents a separate thought about death: the peaceful last sleep of those who have faith; their separateness from the living; the possibility of eternity; the poet as above the ground, looking down, then up into the starry heavens. But as you can see, there is more than one interpretation. This multidimensional nature is one of the things that makes Dickinson's poetry so enduring and widely read.

Another poem we should consider in this chapter is #341, "After great pain."

After great pain, a formal feeling comes—
The Nerves sit ceremonious, like Tombs—
The stiff Heart questions was it He, that bore,
And Yesterday, or Centuries before?

The Feet, mechanical, go round—
A Wooden way
Of Ground, or Air, or Ought—

Regardless grown,
A Quartz contentment, like a stone—

This is the Hour of Lead—
Remembered, if outlived,
As Freezing persons, recollect the Snow—
First—Chill—then Stupor—then the letting go—

From the first line, Dickinson talks about pain. But what kind of pain? It is not physical. "The Nerves sit ceremonious, like Tombs," writes Dickinson, and one reading is that these nerves resemble a group of people after a funeral, sitting stiffly and quietly in a parlor.[14] Perhaps Dickinson wrote the poem at a time when she was "turning inward" and it refers to "a horrifying psychological catastrophe and its aftermath."[15]

It is possible Emily Dickinson suffered from a personality disorder called *schizotypy*.[16] People with the disease shy away from face-to-face interaction, withdraw from social events, and act in ways that seem odd. They may, for example, dress or use words strangely. There does seem to be an odd pairing of words in this poem. Notice the images in the lines of the first stanza: nerves sitting ceremoniously, a heart stiff with grief. The feet walk mechanically, "go round / A Wooden way" unable to stay straight.

With this imagery, Dickinson conveys a sense of numbness, a quality of deadness underscored by those feet mechanically moving "regardless" of where they go. The lines seem to hang together, not only by the constant images of stillness and heaviness, but also by the fact that the poet runs down a list of body parts—nerves, heart, feet—that appear to have shut down as the result of grief.

Examine the third and fourth lines of the first stanza ("The stiff Heart questions was it He, that bore /And Yesterday, or Centuries before?") more closely. Who is "He?" Could Dickinson be referring to a divine being, perhaps God or Jesus? If you think of the Heart as a person stiff with pain, not knowing time or place. and the "He" is Jesus, could it be that the Heart, in its confusion, is asking whether Christ bore the cross? This sudden question appears in the poem as if blurted out in a moment of suffering; it's like the Heart is asking "Am I experiencing Jesus' pain?" And because it has lost sense of time, it asks, "Did the crucifixion take place yesterday or centuries earlier?"

Behind such inquiries lies Dickinson's notion that pain is a constant part of human existence. Dickinson asks us to consider that the suffering of one heart is similar to the suffering Jesus must have felt on the cross. This may not seem like an extraordinary notion today, but in 1862 it was very radical.

Further on we read the line "A quartz contentment

like a stone." Critics Robert Penn Warren and Cleanth Brooks offer two commentaries on this comparison. "The name of the stone helps to particularize the figure and prevent the effect of a cliché. Moreover, quartz is a very hard stone. And, for one who knows that quartz is a crystal, a 'quartz contentment' is a contentment crystallized, as it were, out of the pain."[17] The second reason is ironic and rather remarkable. The poet refers to contentment, but this is not the kind of satisfaction we usually think of when we're happy. Rather, this contentment is hard and occurs because of the inability to respond any longer.

So far the poet has created a scene of lifelessness. In the last stanza Dickinson introduces a new metaphor: freezing persons recollecting snow. "Remembered if outlived," she writes as if to say that the experience of grief is like a death by freezing. First, there is the chill, then unconsciousness (the "stupor") as the body becomes numb, then the last stage in which the body finally gives up the fight against the cold, relaxes, and dies. By mentioning the stages of death by freezing near the mention of the shock of deep grief, the passage becomes a powerful statement about life, death, sorrow, and possibly mental illness.

But there is another reason this last metaphor is

so moving. The imagery of the first two stanzas describes the "stupor." But the last line of the poem carries a new twist, one that provides a context for all its other imagery. The formality, the stiffness, the numbness of the first two stanzas is all accounted for: by attempting to hold on, and fighting against letting go, this mind is defending itself against grief.

FOR FURTHER STUDY

Emily Dickinson wrote many poems related to the subject of death and mortality. To follow are several more such poems one might wish to consider for further study.

A Death-Blow is a life-blow to some
Who, till they died, did not alive become;
Who, had they lived, had died, but when
They died, vitality begun.

***

Death is a dialogue between
The spirit and the dust.
"Dissolve," says Death. The Spirit, "Sir,
I have another trust."

Death doubts it, argues from the ground.
The Spirit turns away,
Just laying off, for evidence,
An overcoat of clay.

***

71

Death is like the insect
Menacing the tree,
Competent to kill it,
But decoyed may be.

Bait it with the balsam,
Seek it with the knife,
Baffle, if it cost you
Everything in life.

Then, if it have burrowed
Out of reach of skill,
Ring the tree and leave it,—
'Tis the vermin's will.

***

For Death,—or rather
For the things 'twill buy,
These put away
Life's opportunity.
The things that Death will buy
Are Room,—Escape
From Circumstances,
And a Name.
How gifts of Life
With Death's gifts will compare,
We know not—
For the rates stop Here.

***

Death sets a thing significant
The eye had hurried by,
Except a perished creature

Entreat us tenderly

To ponder little workmanships
In crayon or in wool,
With "This was last her fingers did,"
Industrious until

The thimble weighed too heavy,
The stitches stopped themselves,
And then 'twas put among the dust
Upon the closet shelves.

A book I have, a friend gave,
Whose pencil, here and there,
Had notched the place that pleased him,—
At rest his fingers are.

Now, when I read, I read not,
For interrupting tears
Obliterate the etchings
Too costly for repairs.

TELL
ALL THE
TRUTH

Truth, Faith, and Reality in Dickinson

By all accounts, although Emily Dickinson became a recluse in her mid-thirties, she was a keen observer. Consider again "Tell all the Truth but tell it slant" (#1129).

> *Tell all the Truth but tell it slant—*
> *Success in Circuit lies*
> *Too bright for our infirm Delight*
> *The Truth's superb surprise*
>
> *As Lightning to the Children eased*
> *With explanation kind*
> *The Truth must dazzle gradually*
> *Or every man be blind—*

In this poem, Dickinson appears to be saying that most truth cannot be captured completely in mere words. It is "too bright" for us to accurately perceive. Real truth (particularly divine or religious truth) is too big, too great, and can only be revealed to us a little at a time—otherwise we would be struck "blind" by it.

Another variation of this interpretation is that Dickinson may be saying that revealing too much of something may not always be wise. At times, Dickinson demonstrated such a philosophy in her own everyday life. For example, when Dickinson first began corresponding with Colonel Higginson, she told him about her feelings of loneliness and terror, about her family and her love life, of her turning to nature in her despair: "They [animals and plants] are better than Beings—because they know—but do not tell" (Letter #261, April 25, 1862). But she also withheld her age, the names of her teachers, and the number of poems she had written.

Poem #1129 repeats and amplifies this theme.[1] Dickinson does not so much develop the theme as reword it. Even though there is no punctuation save dashes, the poem contains four complete sentences (line 1, line 2, lines 3–4, and lines 5–8,). Each is really a variation of the first.

Here is another poem illustrating Dickinson's power of observation and her power as a poet—"I dwell in Possibility" (#657):

I dwell in Possibility—
A fairer House than Prose—
More numerous of Windows—
Superior—for Doors—

WHAT IS THE MEANING OF "CIRCUIT" IN POEM 1129?

Dickinson uses the word "Circuit" in the second line of Poem 1129. Today the word is more associated with electronics, but its first meaning is "a usually circular line encompassing an area or the space enclosed within such a line."[2] Dickinson has cleverly taken a slanted line ("Tell all the Truth but tell it slant") and curved it (Success in Circuit lies") in just the way one might "bend the truth."[3]

But when you pronounce the word with stress on the second syllable "circuit" becomes cir-CU-it, suggesting "circuitous," which means "round-about." (The line might also include one of her sight jokes: "lies" can mean "rests" or "tells an untruth.") By using two words with double meaning, Dickinson underscores her point: If you are going to tell the truth, make sure not to be too sudden or too direct or you might give someone an unwanted surprise or, worse, get an unwanted reaction. (On the other hand, be careful not to go too far, or you may end up telling a lie!)

Another interpretation is that Dickinson may be suggesting that everyone could use a little perspective. "We're always trying to make ourselves look good because we all need to respect ourselves, but if you come at things from an angle, you can often get at some surprises, see more of what's happening in the self and in the world."[4]

Still another interpretation is that this poem may be part of a "constellation," or larger group, of poems in which Dickinson speaks her mind.[5]

Of Chambers as the Cedars—
Impregnable of Eye—
And for an Everlasting Roof
The Gambrels of the Sky—
Of Visitors—the fairest—
For Occupation—This—
The spreading wide of narrow Hands
To gather Paradise—

The speaker lives in a place called "Possibility," a house whose rooms ("chambers") are "as the Cedars," its roof "the Gambrels of the Sky." "Ah," one may say, "so this is a poem about nature." But this place possesses qualities of something beyond Prose. "This house is Possibility, the imagination. Dwelling there, the lady of the manor makes not cakes but poetry."[6]

Indeed, the house constructed here is one of poetry, its front comparable to a real house.[7] "Dickinson committed herself to the power of poetic vision, which was "More Numerous of Windows— / Superior for Doors." This "alternative world of possibility was also "Impregnable of eye." It allowed her to "think independently beyond the withering scrutiny of a judgmental society."[8]

A common theme throughout Dickinson's poetry is the power of the imagination to liberate one from public and personal restraints, power to "transform the self" and "gather Paradise."

"The Soul selects her own Society" (#303) turns traditional ideas about power and control upside down:

The Soul selects her own Society—
Then—shuts the Door—
To her divine Majority—
Present no more—
Unmoved—she notes the Chariots—pausing—
At her low Gate—
Unmoved—an Emperor be kneeling
Upon her Mat—
I've known her—from an ample nation—
Choose One—
Then—close the Valves of her attention—
Like Stone—

In the opening stanza, Dickinson claims that controlling people does not constitute power, but the ability to construct a world for oneself (the Soul) *is* a god-like achievement. Dickinson says the soul is "divine," challenging our ideas about what is sacred. Here again she uses the metaphor of a house to construct an enclosure for the soul. It is a dwelling more adequate for a queenly life than all the chariots or emperors in the world could bring.

Even as the speaker claims "divine Majority" and thus her equality with those most powerful in the "real" world, she declares her difference from them. She uses the vocabulary of everyday life: door, low gate, and mat to point out that her dwelling is not a grand palace but a simple house. Although Dickinson associates power with the enclosed space of the mind, her poem suggests that too much seclusion may not be good. When the soul turns in upon her own concerns, she closes "the Valves of her attention— / Like Stone—."

Just as Dickinson was inspired by pain and loss, she equally rejoices in nature and creativity. She once wrote Austin:

> You are reading *Arabian Nights*, according to Viny's statement. I hope you have derived much benefit from their perusal & presume your powers of imagining will vastly increase thereby. But I must give you a word of advice too. Cultivate your other powers in proportion as you allow Imagination to captivate you! Am not I a very wise young lady? (L19)

"I taste a liquor never brewed" (#214) describes the giddiness of creation, comparing it by metaphor to the feeling of being drunk. (Intoxication is a common metaphor for powerful feelings; for example, "he's drunk with love.")

> *I taste a liquor never brewed—*
> *From Tankards scooped in Pearl—*
> *Not all the Frankfort Berries*
> *Yield such an Alcohol!*
>
> *Inebriate of air—am I—*

And Debauchee of Dew—
Reeling—thro' endless summer days—
From inns of molten Blue—

When "Landlords" turn the drunken Bee
Out of the Foxglove's door—
When Butterflies—renounce their "drams"—
I shall but drink the more!

Till Seraphs swing their snowy Hats—
And Saints—to windows run—
To see the Tippler
Leaning against the—Sun!

Dickinson plays with this metaphor by developing it literally and concretely. In the 1800s poets like Ralph Waldo Emerson wrote about wine, but here Dickinson refers to beer with "Tankards" and to drink not made from "Frankfort Berries." Her liquor (the beauty of the things around her) is even more precious.

Lisa Melani at Brooklyn College suggests that in stanza two the speaker tells us she is drunk on air and dew (A "debauchee" is someone corrupted or debased, usually by alcohol).[9] The speaker is so intoxicated that she staggers. Drunk with summer's splendor, the sky appears intensely blue or "molten."

Just how long will nature continue to enchant? Melani says stanzas three and four suggest forever. The speaker will "drink in" nature until foxgloves stop blooming and butterflies give up gathering nectar from flowers. She equates nectar and its positive associations with "drams" (a dram is a small amount of liquor), and when she is through with that small bit, she will drink in nature all the more. In expressing her exuberance, the narrator claims that angels will shake their "snowy Hats," and saints will rush to see her. By referring to saints and seraphs (note the alliteration), could Dickinson be suggesting that God approves of this kind of drunkenness?

Just as stanzas three and four run through the day's activities, the sun begins to set, and somehow the speaker is in the sky, leaning against the sun. By using the word "leaning" Dickinson creates a metaphor: the sun as a heavenly lamp-post. There in Heaven and inspired with the joy of life, the narrator can appreciate what the earth has to offer.

Compare this poem to the ones you previously read. Gone are the shadows and references to temperance. Some critics read this poem as Dickinson's confident belief that everyone can be saved and that there are more possibilities than those put forward by the black-and-white religious beliefs of the day.

Still others note that it was one of the few poems published during Dickinson's lifetime. Under the title "The May-Wine," it appeared in the *Springfield Republican* a few weeks after the Civil War began. Critic Betsy Erikka thinks this may indicate that

Dickinson was doing her part to support the sick, wounded, and dying.[10]

People love to comment on others' behavior. Probably you and your friends talk about your classmates and others you know or see around you. In "Much Madness is divinest Sense" (#435), Dickinson takes on the restrictions of a society hemmed in by gossip and traditions:

Much Madness is divinest Sense—
To a discerning Eye—
Much Sense—the starkest Madness—
'Tis the Majority
In this, as All, prevail—
Assent—and you are sane—
Demur—you're straightway dangerous—
And handled with a Chain—

Recall that in the 1800s, especially in towns like Amherst, social customs were more rigidly defined. Since most people knew each other, most were expected to stop and chat on the street, and probably everyone knew each other's business. Could Dickinson be railing against this etiquette because it is too confining? Dickinson points out that what may be perceived as madness may really be the most sensible course of action and that what's taken for sanity may be quite crazy ("Much Sense—the Starkest Madness").

Ironically, if you "assent," that is, give in, you're

considered sane by the "majority." And when you do not play by the rules and "demur," you're considered an outcast, maybe even "dangerous," and you must be handled with caution.

In essence what the poet seems to say is that madness is highly individual; what is right for one person may not be right for another. By taking the time to look with "discerning eye" one learns what is important to him or her.

While on one level the poem is about deception and reality, on another it is about itself.[11] Look at the first three lines of the poem. "The second line, an adverbial phrase, is what grammarians would call a 'squinting' modifier."[12] That is, it modifies what comes before it as well as what comes after. To make sense of the first and third lines, which by themselves seem contradictory, you need the middle line. Which one is true? Dickinson might quite literally be saying the answer lies between the lines.

Dickinson once wrote to her friend Colonel Higginson, "I find ecstasy in living—the mere sense of living is joy enough" (Letter #342). And clearly, this was a principle she very much cherished. This poem (#249) speaks of such unrestrained love and delight:

Wild Nights—Wild Nights!
Were I with thee

Wild Nights should be
Our luxury!
Futile—the Winds—
To a Heart in port—
Done with the Compass—
Done with the Chart!

Rowing in Eden—
Ah, the Sea!
Might I but moor—Tonight—
In Thee!

It was certainly not an easy poem to publish, especially in 1891. After Dickinson's death, Colonel Higginson wrote to co-editor Mabel Todd:

> One poem only I dread a little to print—that wonderful "Wild Nights,"—lest the malignant read into it more than that virgin recluse ever dreamed of putting there. Has Miss Lavinia [Emily Dickinson's sister] any shrinking about it? You will understand & pardon my solicitude. Yet what a loss to omit it! Indeed it is not to be omitted.[13]

In Colonel Higginson's comments you get a sense of the morality of the time (just the sort of strictures Poem 435 rails against). As emotional as the poem is, it expresses dreams and desires *hypothetically*, that is, as if the speaker were guessing at the experience. Dickinson writes: "were I with you" (in other words, "if I were with you") and "might I but," hinting that perhaps the speaker is remembering past pleasures and wishes for more.

The word "luxury" had a different meaning in 1861 than it does today. Then it was used to denote lust and voluptuousness. The phrase "To a Heart in port" is symbolic of a lover's embrace, with the sea as a symbol of passion—just think of the romantic movies you have seen where waves are crashing on the beach. The lovers in this poem give themselves to passion; they have no need for compass or chart, the instruments of control and reason.

Another way to read the poem is to understand it as a religious experience. In this interpretation, the lover is God. Christian mystics (people who are believed to communicate directly with God) often describe the joy they feel while in touch with God as rapturous and full of elation.

FOR FURTHER STUDY

The following are some selected poems of Emily Dickinson on the subjects of faith and religion that one may wish to consider for further study.

> God gave a loaf to every bird,
> But just a crumb to me;
> I dare not eat it, though I starve,—
> My poignant luxury
> To own it, touch it, prove the feat

That made the pellet mine,—
Too happy in my sparrow chance
For ampler coveting.

It might be famine all around,
I could not miss an ear,
Such plenty smiles upon my board,
My garner shows so fair.
I wonder how the rich may feel,—
An Indiaman—an Earl?
I deem that I with but a crumb
Am sovereign of them all.

***

AT least to pray is left, is left.
O Jesus! in the air
I know not which thy chamber is,—
I'm knocking everywhere.

Thou stirrest earthquake in the South,
And maelstrom in the sea;
Say, Jesus Christ of Nazareth,
Hast thou no arm for me?

***

Far from love the Heavenly Father
Leads the chosen child;
Oftener through realm of briar
Than the meadow mild,

Oftener by the claw of dragon
Than the hand of friend,
Guides the little one predestined
To the native land.

***

For each ecstatic instant
We must an anguish pay
In keen and quivering ratio
To the ecstasy.

For each beloved hour
Sharp pittances of years,
Bitter contested farthings
And coffers heaped with tears.

A CERTAIN SLANT OF LIGHT

The Natural World in Dickinson

Of "shunning Men and Women"—they talk of Hallowed things, aloud—and embarrass my Dog—He and I dont object to them, if they'll exist their side. I think Carl[o] would please you—He is dumb, and brave—I think you would like the Chestnut Tree, I met in my walk. It hit my notice suddenly—and I thought the Skies were in Blossom

—Letter to Thomas Wentworth Higginson
August 1862

During Emily Dickinson's time, many poets wrote about nature as an inspiration for divine revelation; in other words, the details of the physical word held a lesson about the world beyond. Dickinson's voice, however, was different. Though many of her poems celebrate the marvels of nature, she also writes about its mysterious, even illusory qualities.

In "A Bird came down the Walk" (#328) you get the sense of a bird in motion, hopping down a garden walk, pecking here and there. But this bird is unaware that anyone is watching:

A Bird came down the Walk—
He did not know I saw—
He bit an Angleworm in halves
And ate the fellow, raw,

And then he drank a Dew
From a convenient Grass—
And then hopped sidewise to the Wall
To let a Beetle pass—

He glanced with rapid eyes
That hurried all around—
They looked like frightened Beads, I thought—
He stirred his Velvet Head

Like one in danger, Cautious,
I offered him a Crumb
And he unrolled his feathers
And rowed him softer home—

Than Oars divide the Ocean,
Too silver for a seam—
Or Butterflies, off Banks of Noon
Leap, plashless as they swim.

As long as the speaker is unseen, nature continues on its spontaneous and informal way, allowing her to continue secretly observing. That she stands apart from the scene is evident: The bird has a worm for dinner and it is raw, an adjective Dickinson sets off with commas for emphasis, while humans cook their food, sticking to meat and potatoes, not worms or other crawling things.

In stanza two, Dickinson further separates the speaker from the scene. As humans we do not consider each drop of dew or blade of grass individually. But this bird can take a thirst-quenching drink from "a Dew." Unconventionally using the article "a" and capitalizing the letter D, Dickinson shrinks the entire garden down to bird size, leaving the speaker to tower over it. After washing down his worm, the bird continues his excursion, recognizing his fellow beetle, and stepping aside to let it pass. Still, the bird does not sense its human observer.

Then in the third stanza as the speaker stoops to join in, the bird's eyes "hurried all around" and turn into "frightened Beads." The speaker offers a crumb and the game is up; the speaker can no longer remain unnoticed. Both bird and observer find themselves face to face, and the poem's meter, rhyme and syntax explode. The action in the last six lines is rapid. The bird unrolls his feathers and rolls away faster than "Oars divide the Ocean." With extravagant images, Dickinson renders the speed and distance the bird flies to get home. How different that home is from the human's, as the poet illustrates by using even more fantastic imagery—the silvery ocean, butterflies swimming "off Banks of Noon" and "plashless as they swim." "Plash" is actually another word for "splash." "Plashless," however, is a word Dickinson made up—as if to say that all things with wings are of another world.

"A narrow Fellow in the Grass" (#986) begins:

A narrow Fellow in the Grass
Occasionally rides—
You may have met Him—did you not
His notice sudden is—

A view of Emily Dickinson's garden as it appears today at the Homestead.

Who is this "narrow Fellow in the Grass"? At first, Dickinson makes him move quickly and deceptively; his appearance is "sudden":

The Grass divides as with a Comb—
A spotted shaft is seen—
And then it closes at your feet
And opens further on—

By passing briefly, this creature divides the grass in one place, then another. But this thing is hard to see and the speaker has been fooled into thinking it may be the lash of a whip. Just as in "Tell all the Truth but tell it slant" and "Much Madness is divinest Sense," the relationship between reality and appearances is deceptive:

He likes a Boggy Acre
A Floor too cool for Corn—
Yet when a Boy, and Barefoot—
I more than once at Noon
Have passed, I thought, a Whip lash
Unbraiding in the Sun
When stooping to secure it
It wrinkled, and was gone—

Dickinson describes the thing in human terms: he's a "fellow" who "rides" and "combs" and who "likes a Boggy Acre /A Floor too cool for Corn." The word "Floor" suggests a house, rather than the outdoors, making the snake even more human.

Several of Nature's People
I know, and they know me—
I feel for them a transport
Of cordiality—

"Several of nature's people" (creatures like this snake) know and are known by the speaker. She feels "a transport / Of cordiality" for them. Here, "transport" means carried away with emotion and "cordiality" refers to graciousness, or sincerity, suggesting an intimate connection with animals of all sorts. Yet somehow the speaker and the snake remain distinctly different. The last stanza begins with the word "But," almost as a warning and the speaker feels "a tighter breathing" like you do when you are holding your breath:

But never met this Fellow
Attended, or alone
Without a tighter breathing
And Zero at the Bone—

Have you ever come suddenly on a snake? Were you startled or afraid? Maybe a chill ran down your spine, a "Zero at the Bone." But the word "Zero" also suggests nothingness, an emptiness. On one level the poem is an acute observation of natural life. On another, it hints about dangers that may suddenly reveal themselves. Could Dickinson be using the natural scene to hint that the unknown and perhaps even the fact of death is always with us?

If you think the fractured rhyme and word choices in these poems are an accident, think again. Emily Dickinson did indeed think about these things. In fact, Poem 86 was one of the few printed during the poet's lifetime. It was published in the *Springfield Republican* on February 14, 1866. The editor called it "The Snake" and added punctuation where she did not put it.

Even though the poem was published anonymously, Emily was furious. She wrote to her chosen mentor and friend Mr. Higginson, "Lest you meet my Snake and suppose I deceive it was robbed of me— defeated too of the third line by the punctuation. The third and fourth were one—I had told you I did not print—I feared you might think me ostensible." They had not only added punctuation but altered the way she broke the lines, which is precisely the reason she did not want her things printed ("ostensible" here means "superficial"). If she were upset over a seemingly logical correction, do you think she would not have considered each detail of her work? Furthermore, Dickinson wrote at least two versions of the bird and snake poems. Each copy differs in the way the stanzas are arranged, punctuated, and capitalized. She also changed certain words.

WHAT IF?

A poet named W.D. Snodgrass got the idea of "de-composing" the poetry of other poets, rewriting them in everyday language. His book *De/Compositions: 101 good poems gone wrong*,[1] is a collection of his "decompositions." For example, he rewrote "A narrow Fellow in the Grass" like this:

A Slender creature through the grass
Occasionally slides;
You may have seen him but if not,
Away he swiftly glides.

The grass divides itself in two;
You see a spotted form
And then it closes near to you
And opens further on.

He likes a marshy meadow,
A floor too cool for corn,
Yet when a child out walking
I more than once at noon
Have passed what seemed a whip lash
Discarded in the sun
But when I stooped to get it
It wriggled and was gone.

Many of nature's creatures
Are quite well known to me;
I feel for them a sense of
Familiarity

Yet never met this creature
Alone or with friends near
But, frightened, caught my breath
And felt the grip of fear.

What do you think it does to a poem to have it reconstructed this way? Do you think Snodgrass is serious? Or do you think that perhaps he is asking the reader to consider what makes a poem a poem?

Like many of Dickinson's poems, "There's a certain Slant of light" (#258) uses natural imagery to convey a deeper, more philosophical meaning. Dickinson employs the sunlight on a winter afternoon as an *extended metaphor*—a metaphor that is drawn out beyond the usual word or phrase by using multiple comparisons between the unlike objects or ideas. In this case, the changing seasons are a concrete symbol of how feelings and emotional states change too:

There's a certain Slant of light,
Winter Afternoons—
That oppresses, like the Heft
Of Cathedral Tunes—

Heavenly Hurt, it gives us—
We can find no scar,
But internal difference,
Where the Meanings, are—

None may teach it—Any—
'Tis the Seal Despair—
An imperial affliction
Sent us of the Air—

When it comes, the Landscape listens—
Shadows—hold their breath—
When it goes, 'tis like the Distance
On the look of Death—

Consider the sounds and Dickinson's word choices: the late afternoon light "oppresses" and causes "despair" and "imperial affliction." It's winter, a time of year when by late afternoon the day is ending. There is the suggestion of death in the "Heft [or weight] / of Cathedral Tunes," and "the Distance / On the look of Death." Could Dickinson be referring to the distance between life and death? The poet further suggests death by the stillness in the lines "When it comes, the Landscape listens / Shadows— hold their breath—."

Most ingeniously, Dickinson takes a property we normally associate with happy occasions (light) and pairs it with the sorrow of death.

For Further Study

To follow are several more selected poems of Dickinson on the subject of nature. Some may seem strictly observational, while others may point toward a deeper meaning.

Nature, the gentlest mother,
Impatient of no child,
The feeblest or the waywardest,—
Her admonition mild

In forest and the hill
By traveller is heard,
Restraining rampant squirrel
Or too impetuous bird.

97

How fair her conversation,
A summer afternoon,—
Her household, her assembly;
And when the sun goes down

Her voice among the aisles
Incites the timid prayer
Of the minutest cricket,
The most unworthy flower.

When all the children sleep
She turns as long away
As will suffice to light her lamps;
Then, bending from the sky

With infinite affection
And infiniter care,
Her golden finger on her lip,
Wills silence everywhere.

***

A Prompt, executive Bird is the Jay,
Bold as a Bailiff's hymn,
Brittle and brief in quality-
Warrant in every line;
Sitting a bough like a Brigadier,
Confident and straight,
Much is the mien
Of him in March
As a Magistrate.

***

Nature is what we see,
The Hill, the Afternoon—

Squirrel, Eclipse, the Bumble-bee,
Nay—Nature is Heaven.

Nature is what we hear,
The Bobolink, the Sea—
Thunder, the Cricket—
Nay,—Nature is Harmony.

Nature is what we know
But have no art to say,
So impotent our wisdom is
To Her simplicity.

WAR

The Influence of the Civil War on Dickinson

Tuesday, April 9, 1861: "The conflict deepens in Virginia, and the interest of the country in its decision increases as its state convention approaches a decision," read the lead story in Emily Dickinson's local newspaper, the *Springfield Daily News*. On Wednesday, the paper reported that a portion of a fleet sailing from New York southward had gone to carry supplies to Fort Sumter:

> They say that messengers have been sent to Montgomery and Charleston to inform Jefferson Davis [serving then as Senator from Mississippi, soon to become the President of the Confederate States] of this design, and give them fair notice that if they resist this peaceful movement the responsibility of war will rest upon them.[1]

By Saturday, April 13 "War is upon us." Though the feeling in Washington, D.C., was of "great depression in respect to the war news,"[2] life went on in Amherst. There were houses to let, jobs to be filled and shopping to be done.

Though Emily Dickinson kept to herself, she certainly would have known about the war. After all, Samuel Bowles, the *Springfield Daily Republican*'s editor and publisher, was by then a dear friend. They corresponded regularly, and he and his wife often came to call. They would have brought news to her. "In the past, critics have emphasized Dickinson's isolation from the war and history and the merely personal sources of the crisis she suffered in years immediately preceding and following the start of the war. And yet, of the 1,789 poems in Franklin's variorum edition, over half were written during the years of the Civil War . . . almost 300 were written in 1863, a year of crisis and turning point in the war, when even Union victories such as Gettysburg had become scenes of horrific bloodletting and mass death on both sides."[3]

By the summer of 1861, Dickinson wrote Mrs. Bowles, "I shall have no winter this year—on account of the soldiers—Since I cannot weave Blankets, or Boots—I thought—it best to omit the season" (Lt 235). Some people think that this letter shows Dickinson to be sarcastic and unconcerned about the events unfolding, that she and her family viewed the war as an annoyance, a reality only when it affected the family. For example, when brother Austin was drafted, he paid the five-hundred-dollar

Samuel Bowles, editor and publisher of the *Springfield Daily Republican*.

fee to arrange for a substitute. Others think Dickinson felt "especially and personally grieved,"[4] for many young men from Amherst went off to fight and die.

Unlike other poets of the day, such as Walt Whitman, who directly referenced events going on around him, Dickinson's reaction to things are not always obvious. But, as we have learned from reading her work, they are all the more powerful for their indirectness. According to expert Vivian Pollak, Dickinson did "write a demonstrable handful of poems about the war itself and she was in active correspondence with an Abolitionist hero [Thomas Higginson] for some of it."[5]

During the 1850s, the Fugitive Slave Act was a burning topic in Washington. In existence since Colonial times, the Act imposed severe penalties on runaway slaves and those who aided them. At first, they applied to white servants as well as black slaves and were continually enforced until slavery was made illegal at the end of the Civil War.

In 1854, one fugitive slave case in Massachusetts thoroughly aroused the public. Mr. Anthony Burns, a fugitive slave, was arrested in Boston on May 24, 1854. The next day, he was taken to court, but lawyers on this behalf were able to postpone the trial for two days. Next evening there was a mass protest

This illustration of a slave pleading for his freedom appeared in British and American antislavery publications in the mid-nineteenth century.

meeting at Faneuil Hall, Boston. Thomas W. Higginson among others stormed the courthouse where Burns was confined. Although Burns was returned to slavery, it was evident that this sort of ruling would not go over in Massachusetts again. One year later, Dickinson visited Washington (her father was serving a term in the U.S. House of Representatives), where slave laws were still much discussed. She could not have been deaf to such discourse.

Dickinson would not have been unfamiliar with the comparison of the fugitive slaves hunted down by their owners to deer hunted down by hounds: "Thus was I like the hunted deer," wrote the West African slave Olaudah Equiano in his popular 1789 slave narrative. John Greenleaf Whittier's well-known 1850 poem, "A Sabbath Scene," depicts a fugitive slave as she enters a Northern church, pursued by the slave-owner:

> *Like a scared fawn before the hounds,*
> *Right up the aisle she glided,*
> *While close behind her, whip in hand,*
> *A lank-haired hunter strided.*

Now consider "My Life had stood—a Loaded Gun" (#745):

> *My Life had stood—a Loaded Gun—*
> *In Corners—till a Day*
> *The Owner passed—identified—*

And carried Me away—

And now We roam in Sovreign Woods—
And now We hunt the Doe—
And every time I speak for Him—
The Mountains straight reply—

And do I smile, such cordial light
Upon the Valley glow—
It is as a Vesuvian face
Had let its pleasure through—

And when at Night—Our good Day done—
I guard My Master's Head—
'Tis better than the Eider Duck's
Deep Pillow—to have shared—

To foe of His—I'm deadly foe—
None stir the second time—
On whom I lay a Yellow Eye—
Or an emphatic Thumb—

Though I than He—may longer live
He longer must—than I—
For I have but the power to kill,
Without—the power to die—

There are many interpretations of this poem. Some think it describes male/female relations. Others believe it speaks of Dickinson's rage at the strictures of society that forced her to practice her art privately. But think about the verse in light of the fugitive slave issue.[6] Could the hunted doe be a runaway slave?

Consider this definition of "slave" from the

Webster's dictionary that Emily Dickinson would have used: "A person who is held in bondage to another; one who is wholly subject to the will of another; one who has no freedom of action, but whose person and services are wholly under the control of another." If the speaker in Poem #745 is a slave, he or she can speak only for his/her Master. Worse, that slave has no voice or free will, and can be pressed into service helping to hunt down a fugitive and even carry out a punishment. As a slave, a person is without rights, no "power to die."

Another poem (#77) suggests Dickinson's awareness of the dozens of stories of escaping slaves.[7]

> *I never hear the word 'Escape'*
> *Without a quicker blood!*
> *A sudden expectation!*
> *A flying attitude!*
>
> *I never hear of prisons broad*
> *By soldiers battered down—*
> *But I tug childish at my bars—*
> *Only to fail again!*

As early as 1965, critics such as Thomas W. Ford and later in 1984, Shira Wolosky suggested Dickinson made mention of the Civil War in her poetry. However, most experts on Dickinson thought that she "turned inward to pursue no cause but her own,"[8] so interpretations of her work in this light

WHAT DO YOU THINK?

Does Poem #77 use slavery as a metaphor? Do you think Dickinson sides with slaves in their need to run away, to keep "A flying attitude?" Seen in this light, the second stanza may be Dickinson's way of responding to Mr. Burn's case in Boston and to many other incidents throughout the North where outraged citizens tried to storm jails where captive fugitives lay in wait for certain return to slavery.

are relatively new. One recently noticed addition to that possible collection of poems is "A Slash of Blue!"

A slash of Blue ! A sweep of Gray—
Some scarlet patches on the way—
Compose an evening sky—

A little Purple—slipped between—
Some Ruby Trowsers
hurried on—
A Wave of Gold—A Bank of Day—
This just makes out the morning sky!

According to Lawrence Berkove, there was some controversy over dating it, but most experts now believe it to be written in 1861.[9] This is significant, Berkove says, because dating it any earlier caused many to overlook it and consider it only on the surface. And on the surface, the poem appears to be just like a painting: a beautiful description of the sky in the morning and again at night. According to Berkove, there are reasons to believe Emily Dickinson wrote it when Bull Run, the first major Civil War battle, was fought.

In Line 5 Berkove notes the reference to "Ruby Trowsers." Union men, of course, wore blue. But one unit, the Zouaves, was modeled after a unit in the French army of the same name. They intentionally dressed in bright colors to signify their high spirits and bravery. And although they were popular, their bold tactics and bright colors made them prime targets, and their regiments often sustained heavy casualties. Berkove thinks that this poem is a metaphor

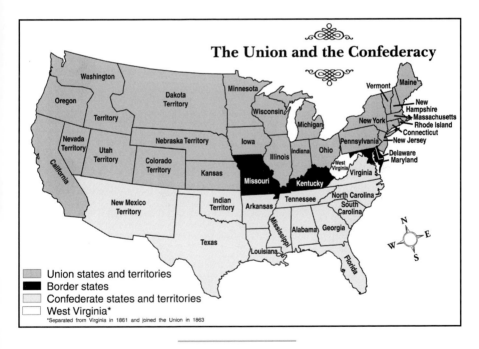

The Union and the Confederacy

Union states and territories
Border states
Confederate states and territories
West Virginia*
*Separated from Virginia in 1861 and joined the Union in 1863

This map shows how the United States was divided during the Civil War.

for the war. "'A slash of Blue!' suggests sword thrusts in an attack either by or on Union troops.

The second clause's use of gray suggests the Confederates (and incidentally supplies additional evidence for assuming a later date of composition to the poem, a date after the war had begun). The verb "sweep" can ambiguously refer to either a crowd of Confederates or, alternatively, a victorious attack by them. "Some scarlet patches on the way" may refer to Zouave troops on the move or, more probably, to battle wounds. The third line establishes the battle as being in progress at evening, but the tranquil verb "compose" suggests a cessation for the night."[10]

There is a lot of color in this poem—scarlet, purple, ruby, and gold—all shades the Zouaves dressed in, and Berkove thinks this coupled with Dickinson's mention of "Some Ruby Trowsers—hurried on" is clear indication that what she is referring to is the war, perhaps even to wounds on the soldiers themselves or the holes created by the casualties of advancing soldiers. "[A] Bank of Day" may be her way of describing how it looks to see many cannons all firing at once to the approaching line ("bank") of troops. "Read mourning" for "morning," says Berkove, "and the last line of the poem sums up the aftermath of battle."[11]

"The Lamp burns sure—within" (#233) is

This photograph shows just a few of the Confederate dead who fell in the Battle of Gettysburg.

another poem we can read with an eye towards Dickinson's feelings about war[12]:

> *The Lamp burns sure—within—*
> *Tho' Serfs—supply the Oil—*
> *It matters not the busy Wick—*
> *At her phosphoric toil!*
> *The Slave—forgets—to fill—*
>
> *The Lamp—burns golden—on—*
> *Unconscious that the oil is out—*
> *As that the Slave—is gone.*

Here, Dickinson refers plainly to a "Slave." This

111

slave provides labor and fuel to guarantee the "Lamp burns sure." The Lamp symbolizes the states of the South, so busy with their day-to-day business that they ignore what their prosperity is built on: slave labor. But a nation that depends so heavily and unthinkingly on its slaves may some day find the slave "forgets" to fill the lamp. And though for awhile, it "burns golden on," prosperity may suddenly go out "as that the Slave—is gone." How prophetic an image. How fitting for the institution of slavery itself to become a fugitive and for the country to learn it could no longer depend on its own light coming from those who served it invisibly.

For Further Study

To follow are two more poems of Dickinson that may reference war in general, or the Civil War, specifically. In some instances, war references may be intended to represent another idea entirely. Read through each poem and consider what possible messages may lie beneath each one.

> *Bless God, he went as soldiers,*
> *His musket on his breast;*
> *Grant, God, he charge the bravest*
> *Of all the martial blest.*
>
> *Please God, might I behold him*
> *In epauletted white,*

I should not fear the foe then,
I should not fear the fight.

* * *

To fight aloud is very brave,
But gallanter, I know,
Who charge within the bosom,
The cavalry of woe.

Who win, and nations do not see,
Who fall, and none observe,
Whose dying eyes no country
Regards with patriot love.

We trust, in plumed procession,
For such the angels go,
Rank after rank, with even feet
And uniforms of snow.

THERE IS NO FRIGATE LIKE A BOOK

The Legacy of Emily Dickinson

If I read a book [and] it makes my whole body so cold no fire ever can warm me I know *that* is poetry. If I feel physically as if the top of my head were taken off, I know that is poetry. These are the only way I know it.[1]

Imagine you feel this strongly about reading, but your father does not like you to read anything except a few books and the Bible. One day, your brother brings home a novel. Everyone is reading it. It is by someone named Henry Wadsworth Longfellow, but your brother knows your dad does not want it in the house. So he hides the book under the piano cover, signals to you when your father is out of the house, and you both read it. This is what happened to Emily

LONGFELLOW'S *KAVANAGH*

We know from her numerous letters and from her poems themselves that Emily loved to read. This book and others such as Henry David Thoreau's *Walden or Life in the Woods* or Emerson's essay *Self-Reliance* were part of the *transcendentalist* movement, a philosophy that holds that individualism and idealism are more important than the material world. *Kavanagh* was published to mixed reviews. "A work by Mr. Longfellow is always a matter of high interest in the literary world, while general expectation is still disappointed in relation to any enduring monument of Mr. Longfellow's genius,"[2] reported one journal (the reviewer's polite way of saying he did not think much of Mr. Longfellow's work). The story concerns life in a small New England town and Kavanagh, the main character, a young Jesuit who presides over the town's church. Remarked one critic, "*Kavanagh* is pleasant summer reading, but of a winter night one would ask a little more of the glow and fire of genius."[3]

Dickinson. The book was called *Kavanagh* and it was published in 1849, when Dickinson was nineteen years old.

As a poet and thinking woman, Emily Dickinson read a great deal. She wrote extensively to Thomas Wentworth Higginson and many suspect he influenced her tastes. Dickinson took her art seriously and was highly intelligent—probably more so than many of her readers and, later, her editors. In 1873, Dickinson wrote the following poem, using a frigate

Henry Wadsworth Longfellow

(a small type of ship) as simile to express her passion for creative writing:

> There is no Frigate like a Book
> To take us Lands away
> Nor any Coursers like a Page
> Of prancing Poetry—
> This Travers may the poorest take
> Without oppress of Toll—
> How frugal is the Chariot
> That bears the Human soul.

Besides Longfellow, other popular writers at this time included Nathaniel Hawthorne and Ralph Waldo Emerson. Emerson was a famous idealist poet. Dickinson had kept a copy of Emerson's 1847 book *Poems* since her friend and mentor Ben Newton had given it to her when she was twenty. There was Harriet Beecher Stowe, best known for her work *Uncle Tom's Cabin,* and Helen Hunt Jackson, who was also from Amherst. Mrs. Jackson was quite popular in her day, outspoken and widely published. Her insights about Emily Dickinson's poetry reveal more understanding and depth than many other literary figures who judged it, and it is said she had a lot to do with encouraging Dickinson to continue her writing. How odd that today she is lesser known and less often read.

As you can see, there were not many women writers in those days, and many who were popular

Ralph Waldo Emerson

followed the convention of flowery words and predictable plots. Though Dickinson liked Emerson, she is said to have been disapproving of Whitman—as did many because they found him too risqué—and may have never read him. She is said to have liked the Brontës, especially Emily Bronte's poem "Last Lines." Above all, there was Shakespeare, about whom Dickinson is said to have commented, "Why is any other book needed?"[4]

Though she is often compared to Poe, Emily Dickinson does not seem to have had as narrow a vision of what a poet should write about (Poe felt that beauty, rather than truth, was most important to good poetry).

DICKINSON'S INFLUENCE

Of course, Dickinson's work has impacted many subsequent writers. Poet and novelist Marge Piercy says she found Dickinson an inspiration. "Like most young writers, I imitated a great deal in my early years. I began with those two parents of American poetry, Emily Dickinson and Walt Whitman. Everything truly American since is a descendant of theirs."[5]

Poet and Dickinson scholar Susan Howe says that Dickinson's work refuses to conform to literary traditions and that she is "clearly among the most

A photo of Emily Dickinson's head stone. The quote "Called Back" was taken from a letter she wrote shortly before she died.

innovative precursors of modernist poetry and prose."[6]

In 1986, a centenary tribute to Emily Dickinson included writers such as Joyce Carol Oats, Adrienne Rich, Gwendolyn Brooks, and Denise Levertov. In her speech, Adrienne Rich said, "I had written a poem back in the sixties, the early sixties, addressed to her, called 'I'm in Danger, Sir,' a quotation from a letter she had written to Thomas Higginson. He reproves her meters, and she writes to him and says, 'You think my gait spasmodic, I am in danger, sir.'"[7] Later, Rich wrote a poem called "The Spirit of Place," in which she addresses Emily Dickinson outright. At that same conference, Gwendolyn Brooks states her admiration for Dickinson's "putting common words together so they make a new magic."

It is not just poets that feel Ms. Dickinson's influence. Aife Murray, a writer and artist, has been motivated by the words of Emily Dickinson to create visual works she calls "Art of Service." "When I cannot express something in one language, I 'say' it in another. I learned to silkscreen in order to move language off the page and onto domestic implements-ironing boards, aprons, tables, chairs-and clothing. . . . My interest is to obscure the border between life and art, so that the viewer experiences the slippage-what is domesticity, what is art."[8]

There have been composers, such as Aaron Copeland and Samuel Barber, who set her poems to music and dancers such as Martha Graham who choreographed her words.

Dr. Lynn Margulis, a scientist at the University of Massachusetts at Amherst has also been inspired by Dickinson. Her field of investigation is life itself and how it came to be. She has been known to use Dickinson's poetry in her talks to emphasize the wonders of nature.

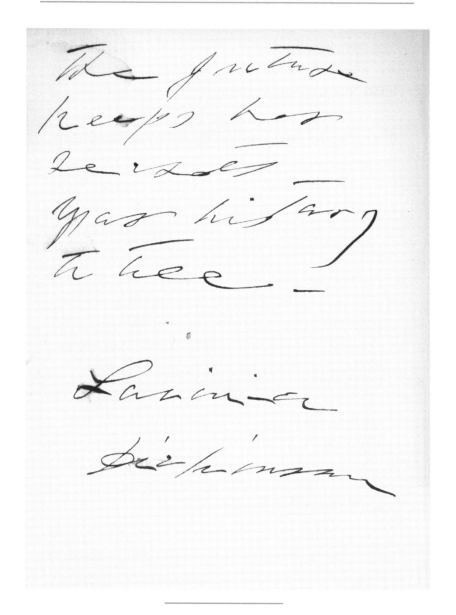

An inscription written by Lavinia Dickinson in a copy of Emily's *Poems* given to a friend. It reads, "The future keeps her secrets for history to tell. "

As you can see, Emily Dickinson's influence runs long and wide. Perhaps Ruth Stone, a poet at the 1986 tributary conference, put it best when she said:

> When I read her poems, these original, hard as steel poems, and I feel the intensity in every word, words used in new ways, bent to her will, then I think she was self-sufficient, an artist whose mind was never asleep, whose concentration recreated, made fresh all that she saw and felt, as though she saw through the ordinary barriers, not as a visionary, but as a laser beam. But when I think of how little recognition she received in her lifetime, and how devastated she must have felt, though her fierce pride concealed it, then I am angry and sad. Yes, a great artist knows and can work in almost total isolation, but it is a terrible thing to have to do. The original mind seems eccentric, even crazy sometimes. In her cryptic inventions, she broke the tiresome mold of American poetry. We still stand among those shards and splinters.[9]

SUMMING UP

One might think when first reading Dickinson, "so what if we don't know the exact date she wrote a poem? Why worry over punctuation or where she placed words on the page?" But the issue of dating Dickinson's work becomes more significant when you try to place the poet in historical context—what

123

did she know and when? Did she have an opinion on the Civil War and write about it or not? Was she just eccentric or did she suffer from a poorly understood mental disorder?

Though she left many poems and letters, she left mystery as well. And perhaps, this is one of the greatest appeals of Emily Dickinson: how little there is about her of which we can be absolutely certain.

FOR FURTHER STUDY

The following two poems may shed some light on what Dickinson saw as the legacy of a writer and the value of literature, respectively. The first poem was composed by Dickinson shortly after the death of fellow poet Elizabeth Barrett Browning in 1861.

> Her "Last Poems"—
> Poets ended,
> Silver perished with her tongue,
> Not on record bubbled other
> Flute, or Woman, so divine;
> Robin uttered half the tune—
> Gushed too free for the adoring,
> From the Anglo-Florentine.
> Late the praise—
> 'Tis dull conferring
> On a Head too high to crown,
> Diadem or Ducal showing,
> Be its Grave sufficient sign.

Yet if we, no Poet's Kinsman,
Suffocate with easy woe,
What and if ourself a Bridegroom,
Put Her down, in Italy?

***

Unto my books so good to turn
Far ends of tired days;
It half endears the abstinence,
And pain is missed in praise.

As flavors cheer retarded guests
With banquetings to be,
So spices stimulate the time
Till my small library.

It may be wilderness without,
Far feet of failing men,
But holiday excludes the night,
And it is bells within.

I thank these kinsmen of the shelf;
Their countenances bland
Enamour in prospective,
And satisfy, obtained.

CHRONOLOGY

1830—*December 10*: Born in Amherst, Massachusetts, at the Homestead.

1840—Family moves to a house on North Pleasant Street. Emily attends Amherst Academy.

1830–1840—Airtight stoves for home heating; friction matches, lamps using oil replace candles; gas lighting, refrigeration and railroads increase accessibility of fresh foods. Demands for greater varieties of foods and elaborate cooking methods increase time spent in food preparation.

1847—Attends Mount Holyoke Female Seminary. Meets Susan Gilbert. Also meets Ben Newton at her father's office.

1850—Kerosene replaces lamp oil; waterworks begin to pipe water to houses; commercial laundries appear with the steam-driven washing machine (still a time-consuming and arduous chore).

1853—Ben Newton dies.

1854—Visits her father in Washington.

1855—The family moves back to the Homestead. On a visit to Philadelphia, Dickinson meets the Reverend Charles Wadsworth.

1856—Sue and Austin are married.

1861—The *Springfield Daily Republican* publishes "I taste a liquor never brewed" anonymously.

1862—*April 15*: The *Springfield Daily Republican* publishes "Safe in their Alabaster Chambers" and another of Dickinson's poems, again anonymously. She sends her first letter to T. W. Higginson and includes four poems.

1865—*February 14*: The *Springfield Daily Republican* publishes "A narrow Fellow in the Grass," inserting editorial changes with which Dickinson is displeased.

1870—Meets T. W. Higginson face to face in Amherst. Pens a few notes to his wife and later publishes these first impressions in *The Atlantic Monthly*, 1891.

1874—Edward Dickinson dies while in Boston.

1875—Emily Norcross Dickinson suffers a stroke.

1876—Encouraged by Helen Hunt Jackson to submit an anonymous poem to an anthology.

1878—Romance with Judge Otis Phillips Lord flowers. Samuel Bowles dies.

1882—Charles Wadsworth dies; Emily Norcross dies. Mabel Loomis Todd visits the Homestead but does not see Dickinson in person.

1886—*May 13*: Slips into unconsciousness at 10 A.M. Dr. Bigelow spends most of the day with her since she is suffering convulsions.

May 15: Emily Elizabeth Dickinson dies. The official diagnosis is Bright's Disease, a kidney ailment, but hypertension (high blood pressure) is more likely the cause.

May 18: Obituary appears on the editorial page of the *Springfield Daily Republican*. Though not signed, it was composed by Susan Gilbert Dickinson.

May 19: Funeral is marked by T.W. Higginson reading aloud from Emily Bronte's "Last Lines." Maggie's brother, along with others, carries the casket out the back door, through the yard, and between the hedges to the graveyard.

1890—First volume of Dickinson's *Poems* is edited and published by Mabel Loomis Todd and T.W. Higginson. It is printed in Boston.

CHAPTER NOTES

CHAPTER 1: I'M NOBODY— WHO ARE YOU?

1. Ruth Own Jones, "Neighbor—and friend— and bridegroom: William Smith Clark as Emily Dickinson's master figure," *Emily Dickinson Journal*, Vol. 11, No. 2, 2002, p. 64.

2. George Frisbie Whicher, *This Was a Poet* (New York: Charles Scribner's Sons, 1938), p. 28.

3. Richard B. Sewall, *The Life of Emily Dickinson* (Cambridge: Harvard University Press, 1974), p. 54.

4. "Letters from Dickinson to Abiah Root," Letter 6, May 7, 1845, Martha Nell Smith, Ellen Louise Hart, and Marta Werner, General Editors, *Dickinson Electronic Archives Online, Institute for Advanced Technology in the Humanities (IATH), University of Virginia*, n.d., <http://Jefferson.village.Virginia.edu/ dickinson> (December 18, 2003).

5. "Letters from Dickinson to Austin," Letter 16, October 21, 1847, Martha Nell Smith, Ellen Louise Hart, and Marta Werner, General Editors, *Dickinson Electronic Archives Online, Institute for Advanced Technology in the Humanities (IATH), University of Virginia*, n.d., <http://Jefferson.village.Virginia.edu/ dickinson> (December 8, 2003).

6. "Emily Dickinson Photo; Between Hope and Belief," *Herald-Sun* (Durham, N.C.), October 26, 2000, p. A-12.

7. Thomas Johnson, *Emily Dickinson: An Interpretive Biography* (Cambridge, Massachusetts: Belknap Press, 1963), p. 29.

8. Dickinson 1958, prose fragment 80.

9. Richard B. Sewall, *The Life of Emily Dickinson* (Cambridge: Harvard University Press, 1974), p. 54.

10. Aife Murray, "Miss Margaret's Emily Dickinson," *Signs: Journal of Women in Culture and Society*, No. 24, 1999, pp. 697–732.

11. "Letter J193 to Samuel Johnson," *Dickinson Electronic Archives*, n.d., <http://www.emilydickinson.org/correspondence/bowles/l193.html> (October 8, 2004).

12. Emily Dickinson, "The Single Hound," *The Complete Poems of Emily Dickinson*, Martha Bianchi Dickinson, ed. (Boston: Little, Brown, 1924), p. 44.

13. "Letter J110 to Austin," *Dickinson Electronic Archives*, n.d., <http://www.emilydickinson.org/correspondence/austin/l110.html> (October 8, 2004).

14. "Letter J265 to Thomas Higginson," *Dickinson Electronic Archives*, n.d., <http://www.emilydickinson.org/correspondence/higginson/l265.html> (October 8, 2004).

15. Martha Dickinson Bianchi in Richard B. Sewall, *The Life of Emily Dickinson* (New York: Farrar, Strauss and Giroux, 1974), p. 650.

CHAPTER 2: HOW TO READ A POEM

1. X. J. Kennedy, *An introduction to Poetry,* (Glenview, IL: Scott, Foresman and Company, 1986), p. 1.

2. Jayne Relaford Brown, "Emily Dickinson Attends a Writing Workshop," *Visiting Emily: Poems Inspired by the Life and Work of Emily Dickinson,* Sheila Coghill and Thom Tammaro, eds. (Iowa City: University of Iowa Press, 2000), p. 8.

3. Christanne Miller. "The Sound of Shifting Paradigms, or Hearing Dickinson in the Twenty-First Century," *A Historical Guide to Emily Dickinson,* Vivian Pollak, ed. (Cambridge, England: Oxford University Press, 2004), p. 203.

4. Charles R. Anderson, *Emily Dickinson's Poetry: Stairway of Surprise* (New York: Doubleday, 1966), p. 262.

5. Ibid.

6. Vivian Pollack, "Introduction," *A Historical Guide to Emily Dickinson,* Vivian Pollack, ed. (Cambridge, England: Oxford University Press, 2004), p. 5.

7. Lori Lebow, "Emily Dickinson: "She don't go nowhere", or a nineteenth-century recluse's guide to cross-culturalism," *Women's Writing,* Volume 8, Number 3, p. 449.

8. Philip F. Gura, "How I Met and Dated Miss Emily Dickinson: An Adventure on eBay," *A Cabinet of Curiosities,* n.d., <http://common-place.dreamhost.com//vol-04/no-02/gura/> (August 6, 2004).

9. Joyce Carol Oates, *Readings On Emily Dickinson*, Tamara Johnson, ed. (San Diego: Greenhaven Press, 1997), p. 27.

10. Michael Myers, "Biography of Emily Dickinson (1830-1886)," *Thinking and Writing About Literature*, n.d., <http://www.vcu.edu/engweb/eng384/emilybio.htm> (August 8, 2003).

11. Ibid.

12. Sharon Cameron, *Choosing Not Choosing: Dickinson's Fascicles* (Chicago: University of Chicago Press, 1993), p. 4.

13. Martha Nell Smith, "Because the Plunge from the Front Overturned Us: The Dickinson electronic archives project," *Studies in the Literary Imagination*, Vol. 32, No. 1, 1999, p. 133.

CHAPTER 3: I HEARD A FLY BUZZ

1. Caroline Rogue, "On 465 [I Heard a Fly Buzz], Caroline Rogue," *Modern American Poetry*, n.d., <http://www.english.uiuc.edu/maps/poets/a_f/dickinson/465.htm> (August 23, 2003).

2. Ibid.

3. Charles R. Anderson, *Emily Dickinson's Poetry: Stairway of Surprise* (New York: Doubleday, 1966), p. 276.

4. Besty Erikka, "Dickinson and the Art of Politics," *A Historical Guide to Emily Dickinson*, Vivian R. Pollak, ed. (New York: Oxford University Press, 2004), p. 153.

5. Anderson. pp. 241–246.

6. Ibid., p. 243.

7. Ibid., p. 248.

8. Alfred Habegger, *My Wars Are Laid Away in Books: The Life of Emily Dickinson* (New York: Random House, 2001), p. 438.

9. Brent Kinser, *The Explicator*, Vol. 58, Spring 2000, p. 143.

10. Ibid., p. 211.

11. Ibid., p. 47.

12. David T. Porter, *The Art of Emily Dickinson's Early Poetry* (Cambridge, Mass.: Harvard University Press, 1966), p. 46.

13. Frank, p. 213.

14. Cleneath Brooks and Robert Penn Warren, *Modern American Poetry*, n.d., <http://www.english.uiuc.edu/maps/poets/a_f/dickinson/341.htm> (July 22, 2004).

15. Vivian R. Pollak, "A Brief Biography," *A Historical Guide to Emily Dickinson* (New York: Oxford University Press, 2004), p. 44.

16. Steven Winhusen. "Emily Dickinson and Schizotypy," *The Emily Dickinson Journal*, Vol. 13, No. 1, p. 77.

17. Brooks and Penn Warren.

CHAPTER 4: TELL ALL THE TRUTH

1. Gary Lee Stonum, *The Dickinson Sublime*, (Madison: University of Wisconsin Press, 1990), <http://www.english.uiuc.edu/maps/poets/a_f/dickinson/258.htm> (November 24, 2003).

2. *Merriam Webster's Online Dictionary*, 2002, <http://www.m-w.com/cgi-bin/dictionary> (November 24, 2003).

3. Stonum.

4. Elizabeth Arnold, "The Art of Poetry," *Research Frontiers at the University of Maryland*, March 3, 2003, <http://www.umresearch.umd.edu/RFUM030103.html> (August 7, 2004).

5. Cheryl Waker. "Dickinson in Context," *A Historical Guide to Emily Dickinson*, Vivian Pollak, ed. (New York: Oxford University Press, 2004), p. 180.

6. Suzanne Juhasz, *The Undiscovered Continent: Emily Dickinson and the Space of the Mind* (Bloomington: Indiana University Press, 1983), p. 20.

7. Martha Nell Smith. "Because the Plunge Overturned Us: The Dickinson Electronic Archives," *Studies in the Literary Imagination*, Vol. 32, No. 1, Spring 1999, p. 133.

8. Vivian R. Pollak, "A Brief Biography," *A Historical Guide to Emily Dickinson* (New York: Oxford University Press, 2004), p. 16.

9. Lisa Melani, "Emily Dickinson—Nature," n.d., <http://academic.brooklyn.cuny.edu/english/melani/csb/liquor.html> (July 23, 2004).

10. Betsy Erikka, "Dickinson and the Art of Politics," *A Historical Guide to Emily Dickinson*, Vivian Pollak, ed. (New York: Oxford University Press, 2004), p. 172.

11. Cynthia Wolff. "Dickinson's Much Madness is Divinest Sense," *The Explicator*, Vol. 36, No. 4, Summer 1978, p. 3.

12. Ibid., p. 4.

13. Melani.

CHAPTER 5: A CERTAIN SLANT OF LIGHT

1. W. D. Snodgrass, *De/Compositions: 101 Good Poems Gone Wrong* (St. Paul, Minn.: Graywolf Press, 2001), p. 81.

CHAPTER 6: WAR

1. *Springfield Daily News*, April 10, 1861, p. 1.

2. Editorial, *Springfield Daily News*, April 13, 1861, p. 3.

3. Betsy Erikka, "Dickinson and the Art of Politics," *A Historical Guide to Emily Dickinson*, Vivian Pollak, ed. (New York: Oxford University Press, 2004), p. 158.

4. Shira Wolosky, "Public and Private in Dickinson's War Poetry," *A Historical Guide to Emily Dickinson*, Vivian Pollak, ed. (New York: Oxford University Press, 2004), p. 107.

5. Vivian Pollak, "Dickinson and the Poetics of Whiteness," *Emily Dickinson Journal*, Vol. 9, No. 2, 2000, p. 84.

6. Ed Folsum, "Whitman, Dickinson, and the Fugitive Slave Law," *Walt Whitman, Emily Dickinson and the Civil War*, n.d., <http://jefferson.village.virginia.edu/fdw/volume2/folsom/index.html> (July 31, 2004).

7. Ibid.

8. Vivian Pollak, "Dickinson and the Poetics of Whiteness," *A Historical Guide to Emily Dickinson* (New York: Oxford University Press, 2004), p. 64.

9. Lawrence I. Berkove, " 'A Slash of Blue!': An Unrecognized Emily Dickinson War Poem," *Emily Dickinson Journal*, Vol. 10, No. 12, 2001, p. 1.

10. Ibid., p. 4.

11. Ibid.

12. Folsum.

CHAPTER 7: THERE IS NO FRIGATE LIKE A BOOK

1. "Johnson's note on Letter 342," *Dickinson Electronic Archives*, n.d., <http://www.emilydickinson. org/correspondence/higginson/jnl342.html> (October 8, 2004).

2. *The U.S. Democratic Review*, Vol. 24, No. 132, June 1849 (New York: J & H.G. Langley) p. 572.

3. *American Whitman Review,* Vol. 10, No. 19, July, 1849 (New York: Wiley and Putnam), p. 58.

4. Alfred Habbeger, *My Wars Are Laid Away in Books: The Life of Emily Dickinson* (New York: Random House, 2001), p. 457.

5. Marge Piercy, "Frequently Asked Questions," February 23, 2004, <http://www.archer-books.com/ Piercy/FAQ.htm> (August 11, 2004).

6. Susan Howe, *My Emily Dickinson*, <http:// www.writing.upenn.edu/~afilreis/88v/my_emily. html> (February 3, 2005).

7. "This is my third and last address to you," *Dickinson Electronic Archives Online, Institute for Advanced Technology in the Humanities (IATH), University of Virginia*, Adrienne Rich, Martha Nell Smith, Ellen Louise Hart, and Marta Werner, General Editors, n.d., <http://jefferson.village.virginia.edu/dickinson/titani c/rich.html> (December 21, 2003).

8. Aife Murray, "Aife Murray: Artist's Statement," February 8, 1997, <http://jefferson.village.virginia.edu/dickinson/maher/statment.htm> (December 19, 2003).

9. Ruth Stone, "Breaking the Tired Mold of American Poetry," n.d., <http://jefferson.village.virginia.edu/dickinson/titanic/stone.html> (December 19, 2003).

GLOSSARY

agrarian economy—An economy based on farming and related trades.

alliteration—Repetition of initial sounds at the beginnings of two or more words.

allusion—A passing reference, without explicit identification, to a literary or historical person, place, or event, or to another literary work or passage.

assonance—The repetition of vowel sounds within words or the rhyming of vowels rather than whole words. Rather than selecting two words that rhymed, Dickinson often used assonant rhyme in her poetry so she could use the most apt word choices.

consonance—The repetition of a sequence of two or more consonants.

1850 Compromise—A series of legislative measures attempting to calm Southern fears that slavery was on the way out, and to reassure Northern anti-slavery forces that slavery was not going to be extended. Under this compromise, California was admitted as a free state, New Mexico and Utah territories were organized with the possibility of choosing to make slavery legal, and slavery was prohibited in the newly organized District of Columbia. In addition, the fugitive slave laws were made more strict.

Fugitive Slave Law—A law that allowed federal marshals to compel citizens and communities to cooperate in the return of fugitive slaves. In 1850, the law was modified as part of a group of compromises to try to balance interests of states in the North and South. *See* 1850 Compromise.

hyperbole—An exaggeration or extravagant statement used as a figure of speech.

idealist poet—Poets like Emerson, subscribing to theory that "matter is a phenomenon, not a substance" because it lets them know "the distinction between soul and world" (From *Nature*, by Ralph Waldo Emerson).

imagery—The written description of a mind-picture appealing to the reader's senses.

meter (metre)—A measure of the rhythmic quantity of a poem, the way organized succession of groups of syllables are organized at basically regular intervals in a line of poetry, according to definite metrical patterns. In English this is by accented and unaccented syllables in the words.

metaphor—An implied comparison between two generally unlike things, usually referring to one object, attitude, or action as if it were another. An extended metaphor is one that is drawn out beyond the usual word or phrase.

naturalist movement—A theory in literature that emphasized scientific observation of life without idealizing it or avoiding the ugly. Compare with transcendentalism.

onomatopoeia—A word that imitates the sound it names.

personification—A metaphor that attributes human characteristics to inanimate objects, animals, or abstract ideas.

revivalism—A religious movement that swept New England around 1850. A renewal of religious conviction and activity, it mandated a recommitment to Jesus Christ and the tenets of Christianity. The movement boosted the temperance cause, which urged people not to drink alcohol.

rhyme—The repetition of identical or similar sounds in unaccented syllables of words. An "eye" or "site" rhyme is one in which words are similar in spelling but different in pronunciation, like "mow" and "how" or "height" and "weight." Dickinson frequently used sight rhyme.

rhythm—Recurrence of syllables at regular or expected intervals.

simile—A resemblance or comparison between two generally unlike things, usually introduced by "like" or "as."

stanza—A grouping of the verse-lines in a poem, often set off by a space in the printed text.

symbolism—A form of metaphor in which a person, place, thing, or quality stands for a more complex meaning.

transcendentalist movement—A philosophical and literary movement popular in New England between about 1836 and 1860. Its central precepts focus on the divinity of man and his relationship to nature.

SELECTED POEMS BY EMILY DICKINSON

Listed Alphabetically By First Line

A bird came down the walk

A charm invests a face

A death-blow is a life-blow to some

A face devoid of love or grace

A lady red upon the hill

A light exists in spring

A little madness in the Spring

A modest lot, a fame "petite"

A narrow fellow in the grass

A poor torn heart, a tattered heart

A prompt, executive Bird is the Jay

A route of evanescence

A slash of Blue!

A solemn thing it was, I said

A thought went up my mind to-day

A train went through a burial gate

Afraid? Of whom am I afraid?

After a hundred years

After great rain a formal feeling comes

Ah, Teneriffe! Retreating Mountain!

All circumstances are the frame

All I may, if small

An everywhere of silver

Angels in the early morning

Apparently with no surprise

Are friends delight or pain?

As by the dead we love to sit

As children bid the guest good-night

As far from pity as complaint

At least to pray is left, is left

Because I could not stop for Death

Bless God, he went as soldiers

Could mortal lip divine

Dare you see a soul at the white heat?

Death is a dialogue between

Death is like the insect

Death sets a thing significant

Doubt me, my dim companion!

Down Time's quaint stream

Dust is the only secret

Each life converges to some centre

Each that we lose takes part of us

Entreat us tenderly

Except the heaven had come so near

Except to heaven, she is nought

Faith is a fine invention

Far from love the Heavenly Father

Father, I bring thee not myself

For Death, or rather for the things 'twill buy

For each ecstatic instant

From all the jails the boys and girls

From cocoon forth a butterfly

Give little anguish

God gave a loaf to every bird

God made a little gentian

Going to heaven!

Good night! which put the candle out?

Had this one day not been

Have you got a brook in your little heart

He fumbles at your spirit

He touched me, so I live to know

Heaven is what I cannot reach!

Her "Last Poems"—

Her Grace is all she has

Hope is the thing with feathers

How happy is the little stone

How still the bells in steeples stand

I breathed enough to learn the trick

I can't tell you, but you feel it

I died for beauty, but was scarce

I dreaded that first robin so

I dwell in possibility

I felt a funeral in my brain

I fit for them

I gave myself to him

I had a guinea golden

I had no time to hate, because

I heard a fly buzz when I died

I hide myself within my flower

I know a place where summer strives

I know that he exists

I like to see it lap the miles

I lost a world the other day

I never hear the word "escape"

I never lost as much but twice

I noticed people disappeared

I see thee better in the dark

I send two Sunsets

I showed her heights she never saw

I sing to use the waiting

I taste a liquor never brewed

I took my power in my hand

I went to heaven

I wish I knew that woman's name

I'm ceded, I've stopped being theirs

I'm nobody! Who are you?

I'm wife; I've finished that

If pain for peace prepares

If recollecting were forgetting

If tolling bell I ask the cause

If what we could were what we would

Immortal is an ample word

Is Heaven a physician?

It's such a little thing to weep

It sounded as if the streets were running

It struck me every day

It was not death, for I stood up

Just lost when I was saved!

Just so, Jesus raps—He does not weary

Let down the bars, O Death!

Let me not mar that perfect dream

Like mighty footlights burned the red

Like trains of cars on tracks of plush

Love is anterior to life

Love reckons by itself alone

Much madness is divinest sense

My life closed twice before its close

My Life has stood—a Loaded Gun—

My river runs to thee

My worthiness is all my doubt

Nature is what we see
Nature rarer uses yellow
Nature, the gentlest mother
No matter where the Saints abide
No rack can torture me
Not in this world to see his face
Not knowing when the dawn will come
Not with a club the heart is broken

Of Death the sharpest function
Of so divine a loss
On such a night, or such a night
One need not be a chamber to be haunted
Our share of night to bear

Pain has an element of blank
Peril as a possession
Poor little heart!
Prayer is the little implement
Proud of my broken heart since thou didst break it

"Remember me," implored the Thief

Remembrance has a rear and front
Remorse is memory awake

Safe Despair it is that raves
Safe in their Alabaster Chambers
She died at play
She went as quiet as the dew
So proud she was to die
Some Days retired from the rest
Some keep the Sabbath going to church
Some things that fly there be
Speech is a symptom of affection
Split the lark and you'll find the music
Success is counted sweetest
Superfluous were the sun
Superiority to fate
Sweet is the swamp with its secrets

Talk with prudence to a beggar
Tell all the Truth but tell it slant—
That I did always love
That Love is all there is
The Bible is an antique volume

The brain is wider than the Sky

The butterfly's assumption-gown

The cricket sang

The daisy follows soft the sun

The Devil, had he fidelity

The difference between despair

The dying need but little, dear

The grass so little has to do

The healed Heart shows its shallow scar

The heart asks pleasure first

The Lamp burns sure—within

The last night that she lived

The long sigh of the Frog

The luxury to apprehend

The Moon upon her fluent route

The morns are meeker than they were

The murmur of a bee

The nearest dream recedes, unrealized

The night was wide, and furnished scant

The only ghost I ever saw

The past is such a curious creature

The Sea said "Come" to the Brook

The skies can't keep their secret!

The sky is low, the clouds are mean

The soul selects her own society

The soul should always stand ajar

The spider as an artist

The sun kept setting, setting still

The treason of an accent

The way I read a letter's this

The wind tapped like a tired man

There came a wind like a bugle

There is a shame of nobleness

There is a solitude of space

There is another Loneliness

There is no frigate like a book

There's a certain Slant of light

There's something quieter than sleep

They dropped like flakes, they dropped like stars

This is my letter to the world

This was in the white of the year

This world is not conclusion

Though I get home how late, how late!

Through the straight pass of suffering

Title divine is mine

To be alive is power

To fight aloud is very brave

To hang our head ostensibly

To lose thee, sweeter than to gain

To love thee, year by year

To my quick ear the leaves conferred

To tell the beauty would decrease

To the staunch Dust we safe commit thee

'Twas just this time last year I died

Two lengths has every day

Undue significance a starving man attaches

Unto my books so good to turn

Victory comes late

Wait till the majesty of Death

Water is taught by thirst

We outgrow love like other things

We should not mind so small a flower

We spy the Forests and the Hills

What mystery pervades a well!

When night is almost done

Where every bird is bold to go

While I was fearing it, it came

Wild nights! - Wild nights!

Will there really be a morning?

Witchcraft has not a pedigree

Within my reach!

You cannot put a fire out

You left me, sweet, two legacies

Your riches taught me poverty

FURTHER READING

Berry, S. L. *Emily Dickinson*. Elgin, Ill.: Child's World, 1994.

Bloom, Harold. Ed. *Emily Dickinson*. *Bloom's Major Poets Series*. Broomhall, PA: Chelsea House Publishers, 1999.

Eberwein, Jane Donahue. *An Emily Dickinson Encyclopedia*. Westport, CT: Greenwood, 1998.

Herstek, Amy Paulson. *Emily Dickinson: Solitary and Celebrated Poet*. Berkeley Heights, N.J.: Enslow Publishers, Inc., 2003.

Liebling, Jerome, Christopher Benfey, Polly Longworth, and Barton St. Armand. *The Dickinsons of Amherst*. Hanover: University Press of New England, 2001.

INTERNET ADDRESSES

The Dickinson Homestead
http://www.emilydickinsonmuseum.org/

Dickinson Electronic Archives
http://www.iath.virginia.edu/dickinson/

Emily Dickinson International Society
http://www.cwru.edu/affil/edis/edisindex.html

Complete Poems of Emily Dickinson
http://www.americanpoems.com/poets/
emilydickinson#poems

INDEX

A

Amherst Academy, 14

B

Bowles, Samuel, 25, 101

C

capitalization in Dickinson's poems, 36

Civil War, 100–113

D

Darwin, Charles, 65–66

death

in 19th Century New England, 11

eternity and, 62–71

theme in Dickinson's poems, 55–62

Dickinson, Austin (brother), 8, 13, 16, 101

Dickinson, Edward (father), 21–22

Dickinson, Emily

birth, 8

Civil War and, 81–82, 100–113

early years, 10–13

education, 13–20

friends, 25–29

housework, 20–22

influences on other writers, 119–123

mental illness, 68, 82

poetry of

A Bird came down the Walk, 89–91

A Death Blow is a life-blow, 71

A Prompt, executive Bird is the Jay, 98

A slash of Blue!, 108

After great pain a formal feeling comes, 67–71

At least to pray is left, is left, 86

Because I could not stop for Death, 58–61

Bless God, he went as soldiers, 112

Death is a dialogue, 71

Death is like the insect, 72

Death sets a thing significant, 72–73

Entreat us tenderly, 73

Far from love the Heavenly Father, 86

For Death, or rather for the things 'twill buy, 72

For each ecstatic instant, 87

God gave a loaf to every bird, 85

Her "Last Poems"—, 124–125

Hope is the Thing with Feathers, 39, 53–54
I dwell in Possibility, 75–77
I never hear the word "Escape," 107
I heard a fly buzz, 56–57
I never lost as much but twice, 62
I taste a liquor never brewed, 79–81
I'm nobody! Who are you?, 44
Much Madness is divinest Sense, 82–83
My Life has stood—a Loaded Gun—, 105–107
Nature is what we see, 98–99
Nature, the gentlest mother, 97
Safe in their Alabaster Chambers, 63–67
Success Is Counted Sweetest, 39, 53
Tell all the Truth but tell it slant—, 34–35, 74–75
The Bible is an Antique Volume, 39, 54
The Brain is wider than the Sky, 36
The Lamp burns sure— within, 110–112

The Soul selects her own Society, 78–79
There is no Frigate like a book, 117
There's a certain Slant of Light, 96–97
This is my letter to the world, 32
To fight aloud is very brave, 113
Unto my books so good to turn, 125
Wild Nights – Wild Nights!, 83–84
Dickinson, Emily Norcross (mother), 8
Dickinson, Lavinia (sister), 10, 122
Dickinson, Susan Gilbert (sister-in-law), 13, 27
diction in Dickinson's poems, 39, 41

E
Emerson, Ralph Waldo, 14
eternity as a theme in Dickinson's poetry, 62–69
Evergreens, 13

F
fascicles, 40–41, 50
Fugitive Slave Act, 103

H
Higginson, Captin Thomas W. (editor/friend), 28, 84, 88, 103, 105, 115

Holland, Josiah (friend), 25
Homestead, 10, 13

J

Jackson, Helen Hunt
(novelist and friend),
117

L

language in Dickinson's
poems, 39, 41
Longfellow, Henry
Wadsworth, 115
Lord, Otis Philips (friend),
28

M

Maher, Maggie, 23
Massachusetts
Amherst, 9–10, 14, 17–19
class distinctions in, 23
Fugitive Slave case,
103–105
Mount Holyoke, 14
social customs, 82
metaphor, 57, 59, 60, 77, 79,
105, 108, 109, 111, 117

meter and rhyme, 37–39
Mount Holyoke College, 17

N

nature (in Dickinson's
poems), 88–99

P

punctuation (in Dickinson's
poems), 36

S

Springfield Daily Republican
(newspaper), 25, 94, 101

T

Todd, Mabel Loomis, 27, 51
truth and illusion (in
Dickinson's poems),
74–90

W

Wadsworth, Rev. Charles
(friend), 28
Webster, Noah, 14

Z

Zouves unit of Union army,
109